Theatre503 presents

BREED

BY LOU RAMSDEN

UK premiere at Theatre503, London, on 21 September 2010

BREED

BY LOU RAMSDEN

Cast

LIV	Jessie Cave
DANNY	John Michie
CHRISTINE	Deirdre O'Kane
NAZ	Tom Reed
BRENDAN	Paul Stocker

Creative Team

Director	Tim Roseman
Designer	Simon Daw
Lighting Designer	Natasha Chivers
Sound Designer	Yvonne Gilbert
Movement Director	Struan Leslie
Dialect Coach	Martin McKellan
Assistant Director	Helen Broughton
Costume Supervisor	Jemima Carter
Production Manager	Luke Girling
Stage Manager	Sophie Martin
Assistant Stage Manager	Hayley Craven
Assistant Dramaturg	Steve Harper
Casting	Annie Rowe & Janine Snape
Producers	Nicola Biden & Vicky Graham
Producing Intern	Colette O'Rourke

The Company

Lou Ramsden (Writer) Lou's stage work includes *Hundreds and Thousands*, which was developed in 2009 with the help of a grant from the Arts Council, and will now be produced in 2011 by Buckle for Dust theatre company, supported by English Touring Theatre. In Spring 2010, Lou was on attachment with the National Theatre Studio, and the stage play she wrote there, *The Half-Widow*, is currently being developed. Other theatre work includes *Gas and Air* (Komedia Roman Eagle Lodge, Edinburgh Festival Fringe and Pleasance Theatre, London); *Black Snot* (Royal Court Young Writers Festival); *The Devil of Great Titchfield Street* (Paines Plough Wild Lunch, Young Vic) and *2004* (Theatre503, short play forming part of *DECADE*). Lou has also written extensively for BBC Radio 4, and is currently under commission to the BBC. Radio plays include *Sampler T6*, *Tree Splitting*, *In Form*, *Dos and Don'ts for the Mentally Interesting* (Afternoon Play); *Blood in the Bridal Shop* (co-written with Nancy Harris); *Lilly's Mum*, *Gunpowder Women* (Woman's Hour).

Jessie Cave (LIV) Jessie Cave is best known for her performance as Lavender Brown in the Harry Potter films, and recently played Thomasina in *Arcadia* at the Duke of York's Theatre. Television work includes appearances in *Summerhill*, *Cranford* and *Sadie Jones*.

John Michie (DANNY) John Michie is best known as DI Robbie Ross in *Taggart*. Theatre work includes *Precious* (West Yorkshire Playhouse); *The Lover* (BAC); *Women Laughing* (Royal Court Theatre); *The Real Don Juan* (Oxford Stage Company) and *Prin* (Lyric Theatre, West End). Other television work includes *Wire in the Blood*, *Randall and Hopkirk* and *The Bare Necessities*. Film work includes *To Walk with Lions*, *Monk Dawson*, *Conquest of the South Pole* and *Truth or Dare*. He has also directed a short film, *The Swimming Pool,* and presented *The History of the Highlands* and *Made in Scotland* for STV. John is a patron of Islington Youth Theatre and has co-directed many of their productions.

Deirdre O'Kane (CHRISTINE) One of Ireland's best-loved stand-up comedians, Deirdre has performed all over the world including the Edinburgh, Kilkenny, Montreal and Melbourne International Festivals. As well as many television appearances, she has released two DVDs of her solo shows with EMI. As an actress, Deirdre's leading roles have included Miss Funny in *At the Black Pig's Dyke* (Druid Theatre Company); Mary in *Juno and the Paycock* (Abbey Theatre); Daphne in *Present Laughter* (Gate Theatre) and Jean in two sold-out runs of *Dandelions* (the Olympia Theatre). On television she has played Helen in *Paths to Freedom* (RTÉ/BBC); Siobhan in *Whistleblowers* (ITV); Rosie in *The Clinic* (RTÉ); Fiona in *The Fitz* (BBC); Marie in *Bittersweet* (RTÉ) and Lorraine in *Fergus's Wedding* (RTÉ). Her film work includes Frida in the Bafta-nominated *Festival* (Film4); Noeleen in *Intermission* (Company of Wolves); Grace in *Boy Eats Girl* (Lionsgate) and Marlene in *Killing Bono* (Paramount Pictures). Most recently Deirdre played Angela in the hit one-woman show *My Brilliant Divorce*, directed by Garry Hynes for Druid Theatre Company.

Tom Reed (NAZ) Tom trained at the Arts Educational School of Acting graduating with a First-Class BA Hons in Acting. In his final year Tom was nominated for the 2007 Spotlight Award. Theatre work includes Col in *S-27* (Finborough Theatre); Maneer in *East is East* (Birmingham Repertory Theatre), and most recently Crowther in the national tour of *The History Boys*. Theatre work whilst in training includes *Gormenghast*, *As You Like It*, *Radium Girls*, *Betrayal*, *Measure For Measure*, *Present Laughter*, *Bus Stop*, *Ubu Rex*, *Three Sisters* and *Someone Who'll Watch Over Me*. Film work includes *Shadows in the Sun* and *Life Goes On*.

Paul Stocker (BRENDAN) Paul graduated from the Liverpool Institute for Performing Arts (LIPA). Theatre work includes *Six Degrees of Separation* (Old Vic); *Troilus and Cressida* (Shakespeare's Globe); *Overspill* (Soho Theatre); *A Conversation* (Manchester Royal Exchange); *Twisted* (Oval House Theatre); *The Golden Goose* (Library Theatre) and *Christmas is Miles Away* (Bush Theatre/Manchester Royal Exchange). Film work includes *Atonement, Mark of Cain, Summer Breeze* and *What's up with Adam?*. Television work includes *Casualty, Doctors, Blue Murder* and *Two Pints of Lager and a Packet of Crisps*. Paul was nominated for 2006 MEN Best Newcomer Award and was recipient of the 2004 NSDF Leading Actor Award.

Tim Roseman (Director) Tim Roseman is Joint Artistic Director of Theatre503, where his productions include *Peter and Vandy, This Much is True, Natural Selection, The Final Shot* and *DECADE*. His other theatre directing work includes *Overspill* (Soho Theatre/Churchill Theatre, Bromley); *Don Juan Comes Home from the War* (National Theatre Studio); *Skittles are a Reason to Live* (BAC); *The Arab–Israeli Cookbook* (Gate Theatre/Tricycle Theatre); revival of *Journey's End* (New Ambassadors Theatre); *A Number* (Dailes Theatre, Latvia); *To My Man* (Yvonne Arnaud Theatre, Guildford/Haugesund Teater, Norway); *You Might As Well Live, Lovers, Così* (New End Theatre); *What Didn't Happen, Karen Morris Tribute* (Old Vic); *90 Minutes* (Southwark Playhouse); *Blackrock* (Young Vic); *Recruitment* (King's Head Theatre); *Our Town* (Warwick Arts Centre); *On Cigarette Papers* (Old Vic/RADA); *Kingdom on Earth* (Landor Theatre) and *Nearly All Sondheim* (Greenwich Playhouse). He has worked extensively in new writing and has developed plays with the Old Vic, Young Vic, Royal Court, Hampstead and Soho Theatres, Theatre Royal Haymarket, Pleasance, Gilded Balloon (Edinburgh), Caird Company and RADA. He was Joint Artistic Director of the Theatre Royal Haymarket's New Directions season.

Simon Daw (Designer) Simon Daw's stage design work includes *As One* (Royal Ballet); *Romeo and Juliet* (Shakespeare's Globe); *Double Sentence* (Soho Theatre); *Lost Monsters* (Liverpool Everyman); *Dolls* (National Theatre of Scotland); *Fast Labour* (Hampstead Theatre/West Yorkshire Playhouse); *DNA, Baby Girl, The Miracle* and *The Enchantment* (National Theatre); *Elling* (Bush Theatre/Trafalgar Studios); *French Without Tears* (English Touring Theatre); *Rutherford and Son, Rafts and Dreams* and *Across Oka* (Manchester Royal Exchange); *Romeo and Juliet* (RSC, Stratford Theatre/Albery Theatre); *Adam and Eve* (TPT, Tokyo); *Kebab* (Royal Court Theatre Upstairs); *Bloom* (Rambert) and *The Stepfather* (Candoco). Installation and performance commissions include *3rd Ring Out* (UK tour); *Wavestructures, Hopefully it Means Nothing, Sea House* (Aldeburgh Festival) and *New Town* (site-specific/Arches).

Natasha Chivers (Lighting Designer) Lighting design work includes *Electric Hotel* (Sadlers Wells/Fuel); *God's Garden* (Arthur Pita/Open Heart/Linbury); *Othello, Pool (No Water)* and *Hymns* (Frantic Assembly); *Statement of Regret* (National Theatre); *Sunday in the Park with George* (West End; 2007 Olivier Award for Best Lighting Design); *The House of Bernarda Alba, Empty, Miracle Man, The Wolves in the Walls* (Improbable); *Home-Glasgow* and *Mary Stuart* (National Theatre of Scotland); *Zaide* (Sadlers Wells/Classical Opera); *That Face* (Royal Court Theatre/West End); *Electric Counterpoint* (Royal Opera House); *Beyond Belief* (Legs on the Wall, CarriageWorks, Sydney); *Encore* (Sadlers Wells) and new works by Rafael Bonachela and Will Tuckett for the Ballet Boyz's *Ballet for the People* (Royal Festival Hall).

Struan Leslie (Movement Director) Struan Leslie is Head of Movement at the Royal Shakespeare Company. Productions since his appointment in January 2009 include *As You Like It* and *Morte d'Arthur*, and previous work includes *Easter, Slaughter City, The Merchant of Venice* and *Cyrano de Bergerac*. Productions at the National Theatre include *Much Ado About Nothing, Women of Troy, Iphigenia in Aulis, Fix-up, Oresteia*. Also productions for Welsh National Opera, American Repertory Theatre, Chichester Festival, Berkeley Rep, California, Donmar Warehouse, Teatro Piccolo, Milan, and Traverse Theatre, Edinburgh. Other recent work includes *Matthew Herbert Big Band and Chorus* for *British Council 75th Birthday* (Barbican, London) and *Everybody Loves a Winner* (Manchester International Festival). www.struanleslie.com

Jemima Carter (Costume Supervisor) Jemima trained in Painting at Glasgow School of Art and then Theatre Design at Motley. Recent theatre design work includes costumes for *Lite Bites* at Riverside Studios for Tête à Tête Opera Festival, costumes for *The Measurement Shop* for Tangled Feet (Elephant and Castle Shopping Centre); *Subs* and *Pay as You Go* for Good Night Out Productions (Cock Tavern Theatre) and *Cells* for Theatre Venture and Tangled Feet (the old Stratford prison).

Luke Girling (Production Manager) Luke trained at Rose Bruford College. He was Technical Manager for three years at the Actors Centre and Tristan Bates Theatre, followed by four years as Technical Manager and at various times Production Manager. Here he worked on in excess of 500 shows, including *The Masque of the Red Death, Between the Devil and the Deep Blue Sea, Burst* and *One on One* festivals. For Theatre503 he has production managed *The Ones that Flutter, This Much is True, Slaves, Porn – The Musical* and *Peter and Vandy*. He is also a Lighting and Sound Designer.

Sophie Martin (Stage Manager) Sophie's work as deputy stage manager includes *Shooting Rats* (Fanshen Theatre Company); *Our Own Little Piece of Shit Paradise* (Oval House) and *Death of Long Pig* (Finborough Theatre). She was stage manager on *Wild Horses* (Theatre503); *Simpatico* (Old Red Lion Theatre); *The Ballad of Crazy Paola* (Arcola Theatre); *Birds* (Hen & Chickens Theatre) and *Stephen and the Sexy Partridge* (Etcetera Theatre). Assistant Stage Manager on *Slaves* (Theatre503); *Painting a Wall* (Finborough Theatre) and *Così Fan Tutte* (Garsington Opera). Sophie also worked as Wardrobe Supervisor for *Romeo and Juliet, Pericles* and *Deaths of Shakespearian Kings* (all RADA Enterprises).

Helen Broughton (Assistant Director) Directing work includes *Le Silence* (White Bear Theatre); *This is a Chair* (Etcetera Theatre); *Two-Headed* (The Rose, Kingston/cornerHOUSE, Surbiton) and *Electra* (RITU 25, Liege, Belgium). Assisting work includes *Crooked Wood* (Jermyn Street Theatre); *Tell Me... Lies* (Arts Theatre, London; also Stage Manager) and *The Lonesome West* (Tabard Theatre).

Theatre503

Under the artistic leadership of Paul Robinson and Tim Roseman, Theatre503 has become London's main and most highly considered entry-point theatre for playwrights, where they take their first public steps based purely on artistic talent and not experience or profile. As a result, Theatre503 became the only theatre of its size ever to win the Olivier Award for Best New Play in 2010.

We aim to create new plays that other theatres cannot make. We respond to the world with immediacy, urgency, potency and power. We produce theatre that poses the unanswerable questions of our time. Our work is nimble, fearless, responsive and filled with limitless possibility. We provide a launch pad for passionate emerging theatre-makers who develop their skills and visions while producing the highest quality work.

Our work lives because of the boundary-breaking intimacy of our theatre. We capitalise on how the uniquely close audience–actor relationship at Theatre503 enhances the experience of watching a play.

Theatre503 is included in *Time Out*'s list of London's top-five new-writing theatres and was most recently nominated for a further Olivier Award, an Evening Standard Award and two Whatsonstage Awards. Additionally, Fraser Grace's *The Lifesavers* was nominated for Best New Play at the TMA Awards, and Ali Taylor's *Cotton Wool* won him the Meyer-Whitworth Award. This is an extraordinary achievement as Theatre503 is a fraction of the size of other organisations and receives no public subsidy.

'Theatre503's commitment to developing the very best new plays is awe-inspiring. Their commitment to nurturing the next generation of theatre-makers ensures the most inspirational, cutting-edge work takes shape on their stage.'

Kevin Spacey – Artistic Director, Old Vic Theatre

020 7978 7040 ● www.theatre503.com

THEATRE503, LATCHMERE PUB, 503 BATTERSEA PARK RD, LONDON SW11 3BW

About the 503Five

Lou Ramsden is an inaugural member of the 503Five, Theatre503's group of hitherto unproduced playwrights selected from over two hundred of the country's most exciting new voices. As recipients of Theatre503's first ever commissioning awards, they will be resident with the company for a year in a unique programme that gives playwrights both artistic opportunities and enables them to be part of the decision-making process of Theatre503.

Lou writes: *'Being on the 503Five has been fantastic. The programme addresses a real need in London theatre. Getting a first play on here can be incredibly hard – you can be an experienced, skillful and confident writer, and still struggle to break through with a first production. The fact that 503 has recognised that, and is so determined to support emerging writers with practical help, is amazing. Production opportunities, development support, and the experience of a great team of experienced practitioners are just what new writers need.*

'Equally importantly, it's been fantastic to just be part of a building. As a writer you're often very isolated, so being part of a group with four other amazing writers, and being part of the day-to-day life of a theatre building, is a lovely experience. Writers can have very limited opportunities to actually get their voices heard in a theatre's decision-making process, but it's important that this changes, particularly in new-writing venues like Theatre503.'

Theatre503 Team

Artistic Directors	**Tim Roseman & Paul Robinson**
General Manager	**Ed Errington**
Literary Manager	**Sarah Dickenson**
Programming Directors	**Derek Bond & Nadia Latif**
Resident Assistant Producers	**Nicola Biden & Vicky Graham**
Literary Co-ordinator	**Steve Harper**
Senior Reader	**Dan Coleman**
Head of Press	**Amanda Waggott**
Education & Projects Director	**Jessica Beck**
Young Leaders Project Manager	**Louise Abbotts**
Development Director	**Jacqueline Young**
Development Officers	**Anthony Green, Hanna Osmolska & Sophie Watson**
Technical Manager	**Sam Benellick-Jones**
Marketing	**Antonio Ferrara & Tom Atkins**
Affiliate Artists	**Gene David Kirk & Lisa Spirling**
Intern	**Shannon Meyer**
503Five Playwrights	**Richard Marsh, Rex Obano, Louise Ramsden, Nimer Rashed & Beth Steel**

Thanks

This production was supported by:

Arts Council England
Wandsworth Borough Council
Richard Carne Trust
Foyle Foundation
Sir Siegmund Warburg Voluntary Settlement
Wingate Foundation
Markus Markou

Special thanks to:

Roisin McBrinn
Annelie Powell
Charlie Westenra
MZM
TheatreDelicatessen
Lisa Spirling
Luanna Priestman
Deirdre Mullins
David Mildon
Wunmi Mosaku
Kellie Shirley
Charlotte Workman
Joseph Stodola
Battersea Dogs and Cats Home
Lisa Martin & Mark Callis from Wandsworth Dog Control Service
PCSO Gerry Coll
Robert Alleyne

…and to all those who assisted with this production after this text went to print.

503Friends

Shine a light on Theatre503

One of the easiest ways to support us is to become a 503Friend. If you would like to join as a Friend or would like to discuss other ways in which you can support Theatre503, please contact the development team at development@theatre503.com or on 020 7978 7040.

Footlights

Juliana Breitenbach
David Chapman & Judy Molloy
Lita Doolan
Georgie Grant Haworth
Mark Robinson
Frankie Sangwin

Spotlights

Rolfe & Jan Roseman
Geraldine Sharpe-Newton

Limelights

Joanna Benjamin
Kay Ellen Consolver
Cas Donald
Georgia Oetker
Stuart Mullins
Deborah Shaw & Steve Marquardt
John Stokerson
Nick Archdale

We would like to thank the following for their continued support of Theatre503:

Arts Council England, Wandsworth Council, Curtis Brown, NJL Foundation, Jerwood Foundation, The Agency, Hamilton Hodell, Anon, Marcus Markou, Andrew Craig, Terence O'Brien, PWC, Richard Lee, JP Morgan, Awards for All, Harold Hyam Wingate Foundation, Sir Siegmund Warburg's Voluntary Settlement Fund, Foundation for Sport and the Arts, Adam Kenwright, Foyle Foundation, The Young Foundation, Help a London Child, Richard Carne Trust, City Bridge Trust, ETC Lighting

BREED

Lou Ramsden

For Ali

Characters

LIV, *seventeen, soft London accent*
BRENDAN, *twenty-one, soft London accent*
CHRISTINE, *forty, originally from Northern Ireland*
DANNY, *forty-five, originally from Northern Ireland*
NAZ, *twenty-eight, London accent*

Notes on the text

A forward slash (/) in a line indicates that the following line or action should interrupt it.

A dash (–) in place of a line indicates when a character would like to speak, or is expected to speak, but either cannot or will not say anything.

A dash at the end of a line indicates that the line trails off, or feels unfinished.

A dash at the beginning of a line indicates that that line connects directly with, or is a continuation of, the character's previous line.

The writer would like to thank: Sarah Dickenson, Giles Smart, Ali Taylor and the 'People With Dogs' project at Battersea Dogs Home, Polly Barclay, Niki Luscombe, Sarah and Elvis Rochford. Very special thanks to Helen and Pete Ramsden.

This text went to press before the end of rehearsals and so may differ slightly from the play as performed.

Scene One

A park in outer London. Late afternoon.

LIV and NAZ face each other. They've been running and they're just getting their breath back. LIV is wearing a hooded top, with the hood up. She is holding a dog.

LIV. Are you sure?

NAZ. *What?*

LIV. I mean, are you sure that it's –

NAZ. Course I am.

LIV. It's just that –

NAZ. Course I'm sure.

LIV. – he *looks* like mine.

NAZ. Yeah? So what breed's yours?

LIV. What d'you mean?

NAZ. What breed is your / dog?

LIV. He's –

Like a sort of spaniel –

NAZ. A spaniel – ?

LIV. No, sorry, I meant –

NAZ. That looks nothing like a / spaniel.

LIV. A staffie.

NAZ. Well, that's a Labrador cross.

LIV. Is it? Oh, yeah –

NAZ. So he's not yours, is he?

LIV. No, course –

NAZ. So you can give him back.

LIV. I can see that now, yeah. God, how – (*Laughs.*)

How mental of me. Here.

She passes the dog back to NAZ.

Yeah, I'm sorry about that –

NAZ (*patting the dog*). Good boy – it's / okay –

LIV. Was just in such a rush.

NAZ. I saw.

LIV. Rain coming. Bus coming. And I just picked up the nearest –

NAZ. I saw everything.

LIV (*babbling*). – like when you're in a club, you know, and you leave in a hurry, and you go to pick up your coat and you grab whatever's there and you get outside, and put it on, and you realise you've got someone else's – you know –

NAZ. No.

LIV. Yeah, cos him and my dog, they're both –

NAZ. – ?

LIV. Brown.

I'm really sorry, anyway. Have a nice day.

NAZ. Hang on.

LIV (*backing away*). Got to go.

NAZ. Oi – no –

LIV. Look, I've apologised –

NAZ. You were trying to steal him. Weren't you?

Beat.

LIV (*laughs*). What? No, I just explained –

NAZ. I saw you pick him up –

LIV. By accident.

NAZ. No, it wasn't.

I was watching the whole thing. Saw you tempt him over with the snack.

Stuck a lead on him and tried to pull, didn't you, but he wouldn't come so you grabbed him and ran –

LIV (*laughs*). You were watching me?

NAZ. From behind them bushes.

LIV. You know, if you're a park-bench perv you're not meant to go telling people.

NAZ. I'm not a pervert.

LIV. No? Cos you'd be good at it.

NAZ. I'm a police officer.

Beat.

LIV. You're not a pig. You look about twelve.

NAZ *shows her a warrant card.*

Nice uniform, Miss Marple.

NAZ. I'm plain-clothes.

LIV. Pull the other one.

NAZ. I know you were trying to steal this dog.

And I know exactly why.

LIV. Oh, you do, do you?

NAZ. Yeah. So why don't we talk about that.

Beat. She throws her hands up.

LIV. Okay. You got me. I wanted him.

NAZ. I realise that.

LIV. Is it my fault he's so cute? I had to have him.

NAZ. What, cos you're some kid who can't control / herself?

LIV. I'm not a kid.

NAZ. No. So don't play stupid.

Not the first dog you've stolen, is it?

LIV. I don't know what you're talking about.

NAZ (*gets a notepad out, reads*). Last Tuesday, 16:00 hours, you took a border collie from next to the gates.

LIV (*laughs*). No, I didn't –

NAZ. Owner was distracted and didn't notice. You led him off and ran.

Wednesday 19th, 17:30 hours, I was in the same location –

LIV. Lot of free time on your hands?

NAZ. And I saw you pick up a black Lab from the north side of the pond.

Friday 21st. 17:00 hours. You made off with an old greyhound, didn't you? And that time I got this gut feeling, you know. Something weird.

LIV. Yeah, *you*.

NAZ. So I followed you home –

LIV. Bollocks you did.

NAZ. All the way out to – (*Refers to notepad.*) Crown Lane.

You live with your mum and your – brother, is it? Number 4.

Backs onto the fields. Big yard, must come in handy.

Your dad's in Wandsworth. The last two / years –

LIV. Hey, don't you talk about my dad –

NAZ. Your name's Liv.

I'm Naz.

I hope we can be useful to each other.

He holds out his hand for her to shake. She turns as if to run.

No, please, don't. I'm faster than you, and I know where you live.

Beat.

LIV. Fine. If you're really going to nick me for trying to steal some mangy old mongrel, let's just get on with it.

NAZ. Oh, so you want me to do that? Escort you home and tell your mum all about this?

LIV. –

NAZ. Let her know you been stupid enough to get caught?

LIV. I'm not stupid.

NAZ. No, I don't think you are.

And we don't have to tell her about this. I'll help you, if you help me.

LIV. Handjob, is it?

NAZ. I just want some information. I know what your family do –

LIV. My mum and my brother are good people. We're / happy –

NAZ. Please – please don't bullshit me.

Liv, I've seen your place. I've seen your yard –

LIV. You're bluffing.

NAZ. – and I know what goes on in your house.

LIV. Yeah?

So what's that then?

Scene Two

Early evening, the same day. The backroom of a family house. It is within striking distance of the city, but quite isolated.

On one side there is a back door opening onto a yard, and a window facing the same direction. Opposite, there's a front window – with a blind drawn down. There is also an internal door leading out to the hallway, stairs, and the front door. All the doors and windows have heavy locks.

One area of the room is laid out with a dining set. And in another corner there are two or three items of furniture – a cupboard, screen, perhaps a chest of drawers – crushed together so that the whole wall in that space is covered. This looks odd, but other than this the house is very ordinary. It feels lived-in, but not comfortable. Chintzy, but not cosy. There are some signs of disrepair – peeling paper, perhaps a leak – but it is not dilapidated.

CHRISTINE *enters. She is wearing a business trouser-suit and carrying a smart handbag. She chucks her stuff down, kicks off her heels. She checks her watch – she's got work to do. She goes to the light switch and flicks it. The lights come on, then fizz off.*

CHRISTINE. Fuck's sake –

She goes to the corner cupboard and fetches a toolkit, takes it out to the hallway. The sounds of her messing with a fuse box under the stairs, just offstage.

Whilst she's gone, the back door opens and BRENDAN *enters. He is carrying a McDonald's Happy Meal box, and eating a burger. He sits down at the table, finishes the burger. Then he opens the box. Inside there's a rabbit. He lifts it out and puts it on the table. He strokes it. Meanwhile, with his other hand, he picks his nose. The lights flicker and come on again –*

BRENDAN. Ah!

CHRISTINE (*shouting from offstage*). Brendan, is that you?

BRENDAN (*resuming the nose-picking*). Course it's me.

CHRISTINE (*offstage*). Good. Get your finger out your nose and tell me if the lights are back on in there.

The lights go out again.

BRENDAN. No.

And on again.

Yes.

BRENDAN *puts the rabbit back in the box as he hears her returning – he is excited about it but tries to conceal this.* CHRISTINE *enters with the toolkit, puts it away.*

You're back –

CHRISTINE. Is your fucking sister not home yet?

BRENDAN. Mum –

CHRISTINE. She's late again.

BRENDAN. Hey, Mum –

He is shifting from one foot to another, excited.

CHRISTINE. What's the matter with you?

BRENDAN. I've got something.

CHRISTINE. Piles? Sit down, for Christ's sake.

BRENDAN. Something that we could use tonight. I think you'll like it –

Pushes the Happy Meal box across to her.

CHRISTINE. What's that?

BRENDAN. Open it.

CHRISTINE. I told you, I don't want you to save me those silly toys –

BRENDAN. No, open it, go on.

CHRISTINE *opens the box.*

It's a rabbit.

CHRISTINE. I can see that.

BRENDAN. I thought Rex could have it. Training.

CHRISTINE. It's got some kind of disease.

BRENDAN. Training log for the keep says we need to work on his reflexes.

CHRISTINE. And what kind of work is he going to get with bloody – Bugs Bunny with AIDS?

BRENDAN. I just thought –

CHRISTINE. Don't be ridiculous, Bren, you don't think.

BRENDAN. Sometimes, I do.

CHRISTINE. Look, no offence, sweetheart, but you're a bit of a fucking tool sometimes, you know that? – and not the sharpest one. Put it out the back.

BRENDAN. I was trying to be / useful –

CHRISTINE. Put it out the back before it infects us all.

BRENDAN *picks up the box and takes it to the back door. He opens the door and puts the rabbit outside in the yard. Comes back into the room as* CHRISTINE *is starting to set up again.*

If you want to be useful you can help set up, come on.

They start carting stuff into the room from offstage. There are three or four solid wooden barriers, waist-height. Then a roll of carpet, tied up, and a bucket of water with a sponge.

BRENDAN. How was your 'business trip' then? –

CHRISTINE. Don't take the piss. It's important to make a good impression.

Assert oneself. Went well, thank you.

BRENDAN. The Brummies going to come to the party?

CHRISTINE. They might take a bit more persuading.

BRENDAN. What? Why?

CHRISTINE. They've a few reservations. I let slip about – you know – (*Points upstairs.*)

And they said we weren't a very reputable family.

BRENDAN. 'Reputable'?

CHRISTINE. I mean, what do they think this is, Jane fucking Austen? As if they're whiter-than-white.

BRENDAN. Well, no, they're Pakis.

CHRISTINE. Don't say 'Pakis', Brendan, makes you sound like a yob.

Come on, furniture.

CHRISTINE takes off her suit jacket and they set to work moving the furniture away from the corner of the room.

What happened with the other lads, then? D'you get through?

BRENDAN. I went to the phone box just then.

CHRISTINE. Aye, I told you to, Bren. And?

BRENDAN. Keith, Paul, Gary, Stevie are all up for it. They'll get a ferry Sunday night.

CHRISTINE. Good. Oh, and let's have the contact list before you forget –

She unzips his top and reaches for a piece of paper tucked into his breast pocket.

BRENDAN. Stevie said: 'Your mammy's organising a party? Your *mammy?*'

CHRISTINE (*as she destroys the list*). And what's that supposed to mean?

BRENDAN. It means you don't normally / organise –

CHRISTINE. I know what it means. Patronising cunt.

I can run a party night as well as the rest. I'll show him.

As they move the furniture, they are uncovering marks on the floral-patterned wall. It is grubby, perhaps has some holes in places, as if something has bashed up against it. The paint or pattern is faded, where something has been scrubbed off. All these marks are below waist-height.

What about Richie?

BRENDAN. He's a bit nervous. Had the USPCA sniffing round him lately.

CHRISTINE. He's such a fucking wetwipe.

BRENDAN. He said security better be tight as a nun's cunt or he's not coming near.

CHRISTINE. *Manners*, Bren. Your cousin would not say that, he's a Catholic.

BRENDAN. Well then, he knows what he's talking about.

CHRISTINE. Ring him back and tell him there'll be plenty of – you know – party fare.

BRENDAN. Hokey-cokey?

CHRISTINE. Aye, that's what it's all about. If we can guarantee him a couple of lines he'll follow his nose here, you watch.

Carpet.

Now they roll out the carpet on the floor. It is cut so that it covers a neat space in the cleared corner. It is covered in blood-stains, but its dark colour nearly conceals this. They set up the wooden barriers around this carpeted area.

BRENDAN. So what we going to do about the Brummie boys?

CHRISTINE. Don't worry, I'll get them. They just need a bit of persuasion.

She goes to the cupboard and finds a video camera.

We'll make them a home movie. A wee showreel of our Rexy, and I'll go back with it tomorrow. Remind them what they'd be missing if they turned us down.

BRENDAN. That's a good idea, Mum.

CHRISTINE. Of course it is, I'm full of them. Why d'you think your daddy married me?

The doorbell rings. BRENDAN *and* CHRISTINE *instinctively duck.*

Shit. Go and see who it is.

BRENDAN *takes a flick knife from his pocket.*

Hey – no –

BRENDAN. I can manage it.

CHRISTINE. Be calm, remember? A firm warning, that's all.

Tutting, BRENDAN *puts the knife away again and goes out to the front door. He returns with* LIV.

Jesus, Livia.

LIV. What? I forgot my key.

CHRISTINE (*looks at her watch*). And where the fuck have you been? Curfew was seven.

LIV. I know. Listen, Mum – (*Stops as she sees...*) What you doing with the camera?

BRENDAN. Just having a little film-shoot.

LIV. I thought Daddy said recording was too risky.

CHRISTINE *goes to the cupboard and takes out a pair of waterproof overalls. As they continue talking she puts them on over her clothes.*

BRENDAN. It's for the Brummies. To persuade them that Mum can put on a show.

LIV. The new lot? They don't want to come here?

CHRISTINE. Aye, and you know why? They heard about *your* antics and they didn't like the sound.

LIV. Well. Fuck them then.

CHRISTINE. No, not 'fuck them'. Despite what you may think, my wee slag, fucking people is not the answer to everything.

BRENDAN *snorts laughter.*

They understand the sport, like us. They've got some fine dogs –

BRENDAN. And deep pockets.

CHRISTINE. With a spare twenty grand in, let's hope.

LIV. What do we need twenty grand for?

CHRISTINE. Oh – never you mind.

LIV. Well, if it's nothing important then we / could just –

CHRISTINE. Did I say it was nothing important? It's very fucking important –

It's not something your stupid wee head could understand, that's all. But if I say we need that money, then we need that fucking money.

So. Let's see what you brought.

CHRISTINE *goes out to the hallway, looking. But realises there's no dog.*

Where's the stooge?

LIV. Erm. Yeah. I –

CHRISTINE. The dog for the warm-up.

LIV. I couldn't get one.

BRENDAN. You what?

CHRISTINE. That's your job, Liv.

LIV. I know. But listen –

CHRISTINE. Your only fucking contribution.

LIV. I tried, alright? I just –

BRENDAN. Messed up.

CHRISTINE. Of course you did.

BRENDAN. Er. And it's the park next to the dog's home –

LIV. Er. *I know.*

BRENDAN. – but even then you couldn't get one? Useless little slut.

LIV. Oh, fuck off back to the – (*In her 'stupid' voice.*) slow rea-ders' group, Brendan.

BRENDAN (*to* CHRISTINE). She's doing the voice / again –

LIV. Come on, it's a joke –

CHRISTINE. We don't do jokes in this family.

LIV. Brendan's a walking joke –

CHRISTINE. Aye, and I'll let him give you the punchline if you don't shut up. Now what went wrong?

BRENDAN. Hey, Mum – Mum – I bet she was caught.

CHRISTINE. Caught?

BRENDAN. Yeah, she's been slapdash the last few weeks –

LIV. No, I haven't.

BRENDAN. Head in the clouds.

CHRISTINE. You weren't caught, were you? Liv, tell me you weren't that brainless –

BRENDAN. Of course she was.

LIV. I'm not brainless –

CHRISTINE. God, and did you remember the decoy name?

BRENDAN. What's the decoy name?

CHRISTINE. The fake one we serve up to the peelers. And I bet you forgot it –

LIV. No –

CHRISTINE. You stupid, / pointless –

LIV (*louder*). No. Look –

I wasn't caught, alright?

I didn't need a bloody decoy name cos I wasn't caught.

CHRISTINE. You're sure?

LIV. What, you think I'm as useless as him? I just –

I couldn't find one good enough, that's all. Not a match for Rex.

I'm sorry. I'll try harder tomorrow.

BRENDAN (*disappointed*). So we're not having a warm-up tonight?

CHRISTINE. Course we are. We've got to get him on form. Brendan, fetch that rabbit.

LIV. What rabbit – ?

CHRISTINE. Give him a taste of blood, at least.

BRENDAN goes to the back door. The rabbit is still on the doorstep. He picks it up and puts it in the Happy Meal box again.

BRENDAN. Shall I bring Rex in?

CHRISTINE. Hardly worth the clean-up. Just take it out to the kennel.

She hands him the camera to take.

BRENDAN (*heading out, excited*). Here we go. The fucking – fireworks!

BRENDAN goes out the back door, shutting it behind him. After a moment, the sound of two or three pit bull dogs barking furiously outside in the yard. CHRISTINE takes off her waterproofs again as she watches the dogs through the window.

LIV. Did you go and see Daddy this morning? How was he?

CHRISTINE. Aye, he was pleased to see me. Pleased with what I've done for the business.

LIV. Is there –

Is there any news yet? About parole?

CHRISTINE. No.

LIV. What, none at all?

Did he ask after me?

CHRISTINE. Of course not.

LIV. Right.

CHRISTINE. And what would I say if he did? That you've been letting us down lately. That my party hasn't got your full support.

LIV. Course it has –

CHRISTINE. You know, if you don't want to pull your weight with us you can always go out there and get a job. With no exams. No qualifications. How about that?

LIV. No.

CHRISTINE. Have the humiliation of no one wanting / you.

LIV. No, Mum.

CHRISTINE. Well then. You're on your final warning. Don't piss me off again. Monday is my night and it's going to go well. If not for me, do it for Daddy.

LIV. I don't want to let him down.

CHRISTINE. Then do better, next time.

Beat.

LIV. That old decoy name, you said – I think I've forgotten it –

CHRISTINE. Paddy Corrigan.

LIV. Yeah, that's it. *Uncle* Paddy Corrigan.

CHRISTINE. Usually enough of them in the phone book to keep the peelers busy a few days.

BRENDAN *tumbles back in, thrilled, excited. He is holding the Happy Meal box. He has the breathless laugh of a schoolboy who has seen something he can't quite believe. The dog is still barking wildly.*

BRENDAN (*entering, shouting excitedly*). Woah! Amazing! Did you hear him?

Reflexes like fucking wildfire. We're going to need a lot of these little / bastards –

Suddenly, from upstairs, the sound of a baby crying. They all stop for a moment.

CHRISTINE. Ach, of course. Liv, look what you've done now.

LIV. I'm sorry.

CHRISTINE. You should be. You spawned the fucking anti-Christ, you know that?

LIV (*cautiously*). Why don't –

Why don't I go up then?

CHRISTINE (*laughs*). What?

LIV. I mean, I don't mind –

CHRISTINE. Don't be ridiculous.

BRENDAN. Someone's forgotten rule number one.

CHRISTINE. Your brother will go.

BRENDAN. Course I will.

CHRISTINE (*to* BRENDAN). Tell him to shut his bake, go on.

BRENDAN *goes, still carrying the Happy Meal box in his hand.*

LIV. You know, Brendan doesn't always have to do it. I could go and see him –

CHRISTINE. You see him on Saturday mornings. That's what we agreed.

LIV. No, but I mean, like –

Sit with him – play with him –

CHRISTINE. 'Play with him' now, is it?

LIV. Not just standing in the corner watching.

CHRISTINE. You know you're not allowed to touch that baby. There are rules.

LIV. Yeah, I know, but –

CHRISTINE. And you know why.

LIV. But it was months ago now. I feel better, really –

CHRISTINE (*laughs*). 'Better', d'you think?

LIV. Older, I mean –

Calmer. I think I could try.

CHRISTINE. Out of the question. It's way too late.

LIV. What d'you mean?

CHRISTINE. He hates you already. Can't stand to be near you.

LIV. –

You really think – ?

CHRISTINE. I think it's quite obvious. You walk in the house, and he wails.

LIV. Right.

CHRISTINE. And instead of this fuss, for once, it'd be nice if you could show a bit of gratitude.

That you have a family who can handle the things you've failed at.

(*As the baby quietens upstairs.*) You see?

LIV. –

CHRISTINE. Now as long as you're under my roof, Liv, you'll obey the rules as agreed.

You'll help with my party –

LIV. I said I / would –

CHRISTINE. You'll not wind up your brother.

And you'll not so much as touch that baby, you understand me?

LIV. –

CHRISTINE. Swear it.

LIV. I swear. I won't touch him.

CHRISTINE. Aye. There's a good girl.

Scene Three

The nursery. It is a bit sad-looking. Dull decorations, hardly any toys or books. There's a cot in the corner. There is a sense of claustrophobia about it, perhaps that the crib is too small.

In the cot there's a baby boy, about five months old. He is stirring, crying – not a full-on wail now, but a discontented, restless moan.

BRENDAN *is sitting beside the cot. He has put the Happy Meal box down a short distance away.*

BRENDAN. Please, mate, come on, you've got to shut up. Don't make Uncle Bren angry, okay? Alright, look, let's try a story.

What we got under here – ?

Under the cot there's a box, with two mangled-looking rattles in it, and one book. He takes it out.

Cinderella, maybe. Yeah? Okay –

So – erm –

He reads unsteadily, phonetically, following the words with his finger.

'Once – up – on a – ti-me, in a – fa – far – a-way – coun-try, there – was – a –

Be – au – ti – ful – gi-rl call-ed Cinderella.

Takes a breather, he's finding it hard.

– Erm –

Cinderella's fav-our-ite thing was to da-nce. She dream-ed – of – goi-ng – to – a – par-ty – at – the – pa – pal – pal-ace – '

(*To himself.*) Fuck this –

He sighs, shuts the book.

I'll tell you a proper fucking story, shall I?

So – erm – so –

Once upon a time, yeah? – there was this beautiful young dog called Rex.

And Rex's favourite thing, in the whole wide world, was to – was to – Grrrrrrr!

He shakes his head and makes a growling noise. The baby is scared and cries louder.

Alright, alright – I'm sorry. I won't do that again. Shhh. Shhhhhhh.

BRENDAN *winds up the mobile to try and calm him down.*

Look, all I mean is –

Rex knew how to party, okay?

I mean like – fuck Cinderella – you never seen dancing like this dog could do.

Rex's parties were the best in the whole wide world.

All his friends would come round, like in their crates, and they'd unload –

And they'd weigh in. Choose the ref.

Toss the coin, and then wash down, and then –

He is getting more excited –

Then they're in their corners.

Rex. His friend. Brought up to the scratch.

And both of them, they want it so much – so much they're fucking quivering, and we can hardly hold onto them cos they're craving it, lusting for it and then ref shouts –

'Let go!'

And they chuck themselves at each other! Like fucking grenades, mate!

And the sound of skulls hitting skulls is like a smack of lightning –

And they mouth each other, and twist round to get a better grip.

And then a rip, a crunch, and the pieces fly – and the air's full of the sound of tearing, and popping, and gristle bursting through skin, and teeth biting on bone –

Then Rex gets fanged on his friend! –

And we got to stop, to part them –

And it's back to the scratch lines – but they won't wait that long –

'Face your dogs! – Let go!' – and the world burns again –

And the whole party cheers when an eye bursts out, and bits of skin hit my feet and there's sweat, and blood, and blood and sweat, and that's when it feels like –

Fireworks! Nature, on fire!

And then, slowly, it stops. Dog is down. Rex wins. Ref's decision is final.

And the whole party's panting and knackered.

And we're counting out notes like they're leaves in the yard – and we got so many, so much, we can make this place into a fucking palace. Mend the roof – fix the lights – paint the walls – and stay here for always. You and me, mate, happily ever.

The baby is quieter now. The mobile has wound down and stopped. On the floor beside the crib, the Happy Meal box has started to leak its contents. The rabbit's blood oozes out and spreads quietly.

Look at you – so cute, wee man, I could just –

I could just eat you up. I could nibble one of them little fingers off, yeah, I could!

Yeah, I could.

The blood soaks the bare floorboards.

Scene Four

Wednesday. The next night.

LIV *and* NAZ *are in a field at the back of* LIV*'s house.* NAZ*'s dog is nearby, off his lead.* NAZ *has an old cuddly toy – a white rabbit – stuffed into his pocket.* LIV *is jumpy, anxious.*

NAZ. Told you I knew where you / lived.

LIV. If my mum sees me with / you –

NAZ. What's the / matter?

LIV. – she'll kick my head in.

NAZ. Just a man walking his dog over the / field –

LIV. And waving at me in the / house?

NAZ. Cos I thought we were friends.

LIV. Yeah, fuck you.

NAZ (*to the dog, about to throw the rabbit toy*). Here, fetch / it! –

LIV (*stopping him*). Oi, no – get that stupid thing over here before they see.

LIV *pulls* NAZ *over to a spot where they're hidden from the house, and crouches down.* NAZ *calls the dog to heel and it comes back to him.*

So?

NAZ. You didn't turn up for our meeting this morning.

LIV. I don't know what you're / talking about –

NAZ. We made a deal, didn't we? I let you go, you find out when the next fight's happening.

LIV. Did I say that?

NAZ. Yeah, you did. So –

LIV. What can I tell you? There isn't one.

NAZ. Don't give me that. I know they're gearing up to something.

Not a cheep from your family for months, and now you're out stealing stooges?

LIV. 'Stooges'? What you talking about?

NAZ. Give your dogs a taste of blood, is it? Warm them up –

LIV. We don't have meets without my dad.

NAZ. But your mum's a capable lady. Saw her sorting out equipment the other day. Making sure you got the rules covered.

Scales for a weigh-in. Rule number two.

LIV. Don't know what you're on about –

NAZ. Buckets for a wash-down. Rule number five.

LIV. She was just having a clear out.

NAZ. Clean towels. Sponges. Leaving nothing unsorted.

LIV. This how you normally do investigations? Intimidating girls in the dark?

NAZ. Liv, I know something's on the cards.

LIV. There isn't.

NAZ. So you might as well tell me –

LIV. No.

NAZ. When is it?

Beat. LIV *plays 'defeated'* –

LIV. Okay, look –

I don't know about party dates, alright? Our ref picks the day. So –

If I give you his name, will you promise to fuck off?

NAZ. Come on then. (*Taking out a pen and notebook.*)

LIV. Bloke who usually referees our shows is called Uncle Paddy Corrigan.

NAZ (*scribbling*). Paddy –

LIV. It's 'Uncle' Paddy. Corrigan. Go after him.

NAZ. I need his address.

LIV. Derry, somewhere.

NAZ. A physical description.

LIV. Big bloke. Muscles. Tattoos. *Loads* of tattoos.

NAZ. Got any pictures?

LIV. Cameras not allowed in the pit.

NAZ. It's not much to go on.

LIV *shrugs*.

Fine. I'll follow it up.

LIV. So you'll leave me alone now.

NAZ. No, I want the rest. A name's not enough. I want to know when.

LIV. For fuck's sake –

NAZ. You can't live in that house and have no idea what they're planning.

LIV. Well, I don't, alright? So you can go.

Beat.

NAZ. Okay, I get it, so you're trying to be loyal. And that's very admirable.

But your family don't deserve that, you know.

I read your mum's file. Suspended sentence for trying to glass some old woman in the pub? Nice of her –

LIV. *That was an accident.*

NAZ. And your brother's a brainless little dealer who's been up for animal cruelty.

LIV. So what?

NAZ. So why you protecting him? When he could turn on you?

LIV. It's just a few stupid dogs. He'd never hurt a person.

And you needn't lay into my family. I'm one of them.

NAZ. No, you're better than them. I think you're a good person.

LIV (*laughs*). I'm not falling for that shit.

NAZ. I saw you in the park yesterday. Picking up that dummy the little kid dropped –

LIV. I don't remember.

NAZ. And when I was chasing you I could have sworn you slowed down.

Making out like you were looking at these women with the prams but I think –

I think you wanted to get caught.

LIV (*laughs*). Oh, you reckon?

NAZ. Help me, come on.

LIV. No. I won't. Now fuck off.

Beat. He is beginning to get impatient.

NAZ. Alright. Fine. We talked about what'd happen if you didn't cooperate.

I'm going to have to charge you with theft.

How'd you like a year getting kicked around in Holloway?

LIV. A year? For nicking a few mutts?

NAZ. At least four months on a DTO.

LIV. Go on then, let's go. Charge me.

NAZ. I will.

LIV. Except you've said that three times now. And you still haven't.

I know you don't want to take me in.

NAZ. Because I'm trying to give you a / chance –

LIV. No, because then they'll think you're on to them. And they'll lie low.

And you don't want that, do you? Cos then you miss out on the big prize.

Catching a whole load of them in the act. Isn't that it?

NAZ. –

LIV. Yeah, it is.

NAZ. Alright, look –

What d'you want?

LIV. You got nothing I want.

NAZ. Money?

LIV. No.

NAZ. Drugs? I can get you drugs.

LIV (*laughs*). No, *I* can get *you* drugs.

NAZ. Protection. A safe house.

LIV. I'm safe in my own house –

NAZ. We'll get you out of / there.

LIV. Oh, and you think I'll just / leave?

NAZ. I'll help / you –

LIV. And abandon my baby?

NAZ. Your what?

Beat.

LIV. My –

NAZ. You've got a baby?

LIV. I thought you knew that.

NAZ. No. I mean –

I never seen you out with –

LIV. So?

NAZ. Don't you go out for walks and / that?

LIV. No. None of your business. No.

And I don't see what the big deal is.

I've got a kid. So what? And I'm not just going to leave him with them, am I?

NAZ. Fuck, no. Course. I understand that.

LIV. Good.

NAZ. Yeah, I –

I got a daughter myself.

NAZ's dog is now at his feet, looking for attention. He strokes it. His tone softens.

I mean, of course you're not going to leave him. You love him, don't you, you'd do anything for him. Fight to the death –

LIV. That's right.

NAZ. Yeah, that's completely natural. So how about –

How about, you help us, and we'll get you both out of there.

Set you up in, like – a refuge.

There's a cracking place we work with, just for mums and babies.

It's brand new. All sort of – light. Airy –

LIV. I got air here, thanks.

NAZ. – and there's this one room that's like Santa's grotto – no kidding – toys, floor to ceiling. Rattles, and bears, and music, and mirrors, and storybooks.

Babies' paradise.

LIV. I'm not interested.

NAZ. Really friendly atmosphere. Loads of young mums.

LIV. –

NAZ. You get your own room –

LIV. Oh, what, so I'd *live* there?

NAZ. Not for ever, no.

LIV. Exactly, so –

NAZ. So you'd have to get your own place some time. But we'll sort you out with that as well.

LIV. I'm going now, alright?

NAZ. I know people at the council. I'll get you settled. Your own flat.

LIV. I'm not interested.

NAZ. Yeah, I think you are –

LIV. I'm going.

NAZ. – cos you said that three times now. And you're still here.

Beat.

LIV. You got it wrong. I'm only staying to make sure you sod off.

NAZ. That right?

LIV. And it's a stupid thing to try and bribe me with. A fucking council flat?

NAZ. Yeah, your own space –

LIV. My own responsibility. Bills. Maintenance.

NAZ. Independence.

LIV. Furniture. I got nothing. Not even like a bed or –

NAZ. You'd find one.

LIV. A cot – I'd need –

NAZ. Sure your friends would help you out.

LIV. I haven't got any friends. (*Backing away a little as the dog comes to her.*) Will you tell this thing to sod / off –

NAZ. You can make some. Go out and have fun.

LIV. With no money? And I couldn't get a job.

NAZ. We'll help you get one.

LIV. You think I need the humiliation of no one wanting me?

NAZ. People'll want you. Your baby will want you –

> LIV *laughs, to herself.*

> Yeah, and he could have you, couldn't he? All to himself.

LIV. Not sure he'd like that.

NAZ. Why not? Course he would. Some proper time together.

> Bet you don't get much of that in there. With the dogs, and your brother, and your rabid old mum, eh?

> You'll do stuff with him. Play with him. Trips out.

LIV (*she shakes her head*). Couldn't look after him on my own.

NAZ. Course you could –

LIV. No way, I'm just a –

NAZ. –

> You told me yesterday you weren't a kid.

> *Beat.* NAZ*'s dog nudges* LIV, *trying to get her attention. She backs away again.*

LIV. Look, I told you, you got to control your mutt.

NAZ. What's the matter? He just likes you.

LIV. He doesn't like me. I tried to – you know.

NAZ. So maybe he's forgiven you. Stroke him.

LIV. Er, we don't *stroke* dogs.

> NAZ *hands* LIV *the rabbit toy.*

NAZ. Chuck that for him then.

LIV (*looking at the battered rabbit*). What the fuck – ?

NAZ. Think it's meant to be a rabbit. It was my daughter's, then she did surgery on it.

> She wants to be a vet.

LIV. Or a butcher, maybe.

NAZ *smiles.*

NAZ. That a joke? Didn't think your family would be jokers.

LIV *shrugs.*

Instead of throwing the toy, she hugs it close. He notices this.

Liv, when's their party happening? Tell me –

LIV *shakes her head.*

Okay, fine. You need some time. I understand that.

So – here's my number –

He scribbles a number down on a piece of paper, offers it.

You ring me when you've had a think about it.

LIV. My mum'll find it.

NAZ. Hide it.

He puts it in her hand.

LIV. Hide it up your arse –

NAZ *(leaving).* Oh, and you can keep that if you want – (*The toy.*) Give it to your kid.

LIV. He doesn't need your cast-offs.

We don't want nothing from you –

But he's gone. She stands for a moment, clutching the toy, looking at the note.

Scene Five

That night or early morning. The nursery. The baby is restless.

LIV *enters. Cautiously, creeping, afraid. She hovers nervously by the door for a few moments, scared of being found, wondering if she can do this. Then she carefully takes a few steps closer. Breathless. Nervous. She looks into the cot. She sees the baby.*

LIV. Hello. It's me, I'm your – I'm your –

Remember?

Okay and you need to shush now, yeah? You're not going to tell them I'm here, are you? – Just between you and me.

She produces the toy from NAZ. *It is cleaner now. She shows it to the baby and he quietens a little.*

I – erm – I got you a present. It's not much but.

I saw it and I thought of you. Peace offering, you know, cos of –

You like it?

She crouches by the cot and wiggles it around. The baby giggles. LIV *is surprised and delighted.*

(*Relaxing.*) Yeah, you like him, don't you? So what we going to call him then?

Shall we call him – (*In her 'stupid' voice.*) Bren-dan? –

The baby giggles.

– Yeah, you think that's funny? I told them it was funny – they got no sense of humour, have they? Not like me and you.

She puts the toy down in the cot and lets him play with it. He gurgles happily.

What d'you reckon, you want more toys like him? Loads of them, I mean, like –

Like Santa's grotto. Floor to ceiling. Imagine that.

And we could play all day long, couldn't we?

Do you think – ?

Do you think we could – ?

Beat. Then, nervously, she reaches out to touch him – carefully, slowly, as if he's on fire and might burn her fingertips. She strokes him. She is amazed and delighted that he doesn't cry at her touch.

Then she decides: she wants to try and pick him up. She braces herself, reaches out to him. Slowly, slowly. She has an awkward grasp on him. She starts to lift him out of the cot, and for a moment it's working. But then, frightened by her uncertain hold, the baby starts to cry.

No – no, you're right – I'm sorry! – I can't –

(*Putting him down.*) I shouldn't –

Oh God shhh – please, shhhhh – look at this – (*Waving the rabbit toy again.*)

She looks anxiously to the door, aware that BRENDAN *might arrive any moment. She wonders if she should make a run for it. Then –*

At the last second, as she's about to lose her nerve, the crying stops.

LIV *looks back to the cot, unable to believe what she's managed to do. Slowly, the baby calms completely. He giggles again. She goes back to stroking him. Gazes at him. Amazed.*

Scene Six

Two days later. Friday. Lunchtime in the house.

CHRISTINE *has just arrived home from another business trip. She has returned happy, upbeat, and with lots to do – which she busies herself with as* BRENDAN *stands by the window, fuming with anger.*

BRENDAN. She's been in there, Mum. The last two fucking nights.

Moving stuff. Messing around.

Thought it was just me at first. Thought I was going mental. But now I got proof.

She's broken every rule in the book –

CHRISTINE. Aren't you going to ask me how the meeting was?

BRENDAN. Rule number one:

Liv to have *no access to the baby* apart from one hour per week, 10 a.m. to 11 a.m, Saturdays. Rule number two: Liv not to enter the nursery at any other time, and never unsupervised.

CHRISTINE. So you don't want to know my news?

BRENDAN. Rule number four: The baby to be washed down by Brendan, and wear what Brendan shall decide. Not *her* fucking choice of socks –

He takes a pair of baby's socks from his pocket, chucks them on the floor.

Brendan's decision shall be final.

CHRISTINE. Fine. Hold that –

She gives him one end of a tape measure, and starts to measure a space in the room.

BRENDAN. Rule number eight: Nothing to be taken into the nursery and the baby not to be tampered with at any point.

Rule number nine: No *stories* to be read after 8 p.m., in case of nightmares.

He takes out the book of fairy stories – it is now ripped up and mangled.

CHRISTINE (*to herself*). Not big enough.

She wraps up the tape measure.

BRENDAN. The regulations are very fucking clear. But she's breaking them, Mum.

CHRISTINE. Then you should have told her that, sweetheart.

BRENDAN. I tried to this morning.

And you know what? – She gave me the fucking finger.

CHRISTINE. Brendan, look –

BRENDAN. Just ran out with that stupid – toy she's got –

CHRISTINE. – this really doesn't matter now.

She goes to the table and starts writing out a list of names and numbers.

BRENDAN. Course it matters. It's the only thing that matters.

It's my territory. And this is an invasion. It's a deliberate fucking declaration of war.

She wants to take over, doesn't she?

CHRISTINE. Ach, she doesn't. She knows she can't manage on her own.

BRENDAN. And I don't know why you're not bothered. She swore to you she wouldn't go in there.

CHRISTINE. Well, maybe I've got bigger things to think about today.

BRENDAN (*staring out the window*). Why's she need to go for 'some air', anyway?

CHRISTINE. The Brummie boys, Bren –

BRENDAN (*still looking out the window*). We got air in here.

CHRISTINE. Loved the tape. Very impressed with our Rex. *And* –

BRENDAN. –

CHRISTINE. They want to bring their heavy dogs here Monday night.

BRENDAN (*uninterested*). Right.

CHRISTINE. They're coming to the party, for fuck's sake! We got a contract with them!

It's going to be the biggest show we've ever held. We'll have to move the action out to the garage – won't get fourteen-foot scratch lines in here –

And I'll need you to go and do a wee ring-around – (*Finishes her note.*) same boys as before but just let them know the order might have to change.

Here – names and numbers, and I've written down what to say.

Remind them, 8 for 8.30. No latecomers.

She unzips his jacket and goes to tuck the paper in his breast pocket.

Oh, and tell Richie security will be tight as a nun's arse. I'm in charge and I will personally make sure –

She stops as she sees something on his top.

What's – ? Brendan –

BRENDAN (*still staring out the window*). Yeah, I got it. Nun's arse –

CHRISTINE. What the hell –

She unzips his top properly. There is blood down the front of his T-shirt underneath.

BRENDAN. Oh, it's nothing.

CHRISTINE. What happened?

Oh my God – did the dogs – ?

BRENDAN. No –

CHRISTINE. Are the dogs okay?

BRENDAN. Fine. Leave it.

CHRISTINE. I will not leave it. What did you do?

BRENDAN. My job, alright? I did my job.

Stupid old cunt was asking for it –

CHRISTINE. What stupid old / cunt?

BRENDAN. Should have fucking killed him when I had / the chance –

CHRISTINE. Brendan, tell me what happened.

Beat. BRENDAN *tries to be calm.*

BRENDAN. Was doing a security check while you were out –

CHRISTINE. Aye, I asked you to. And?

BRENDAN. And I found this old bloke, round the back of the yard.

CHRISTINE. 'Bloke'? What kind of – ?

BRENDAN. Slumped down. Next to the fence.

CHRISTINE. Oh God –

BRENDAN. Trying to chuck chips into Steel's cage.

CHRISTINE. Bren, why the fuck didn't you call me?

BRENDAN. Cos it wasn't a problem.

CHRISTINE. Jesus –

BRENDAN. I can deal with these things.

CHRISTINE. You can't. Was he a peeler?

BRENDAN. No way.

CHRISTINE. RSPCA? A journalist –

BRENDAN. None of them, no. Was just some tramp.

CHRISTINE. A what?

BRENDAN. Yeah, and give him a firm warning, like you said.

CHRISTINE. What did you do?

BRENDAN. Thrashed him with my belt. Sliced him up a bit –

CHRISTINE. 'Sliced him up'?

BRENDAN. Yeah, and then I got him by / the hand –

CHRISTINE. Are you away in the fucking head? You stupid
    bloody –

BRENDAN. What?

    I thought you'd be pleased –

CHRISTINE. Pleased? You battered a stranger in our own yard?
    We'll have the cops round –

BRENDAN. No we won't.

CHRISTINE. Asking questions –

BRENDAN. No.

CHRISTINE. Poking about. I'll have to call off my party.

BRENDAN. Mum, he was shitfaced –

CHRISTINE. Oh God –

BRENDAN. Fucking stocious. He won't remember –

CHRISTINE. –

BRENDAN. And what was I meant to do? You told me to check
    for interferers –

CHRISTINE. I didn't tell you to draw blood, you brainless child.

BRENDAN. Oi, it wasn't my fault.

CHRISTINE (*a deep breath, to herself*). Okay – calm – I just need
    to think –

BRENDAN. Smelly old cunt deserved everything he got.

CHRISTINE. –

BRENDAN. He was trespassing, Mum. That's not right. I told him –

CHRISTINE *turns her back on* BRENDAN *and doesn't notice as he takes something from his pocket. It's the top half of a severed finger. He fiddles with it as he talks.*

I gave him a fucking warning. I said, 'This is *my* place.'

CHRISTINE (*to herself*). If he was plastered he might not remember –

BRENDAN. But he just started mouthing off again. Disrespecting me.

CHRISTINE (*to herself*). Might not even know your face.

BRENDAN. Why don't people respect me any more? Respect my fucking territory?

CHRISTINE (*to herself*). And we could always claim self-defence.

BRENDAN. Why's everyone seem to think I'm so stupid I'm not going to notice when they're breaking the sodding rules – (*Puts the finger back in his pocket.*) –

They can't just walk over me, Mum. Pretend I don't exist.

CHRISTINE (*turning back to* BRENDAN). Okay, it'll be okay.

BRENDAN. It's not okay. I got rights.

CHRISTINE. If you keep yourself calm –

BRENDAN. She can't take what's mine –

CHRISTINE. 'She'?

BRENDAN. I got rights.

CHRISTINE (*laughs*). Don't tell me this is / about –

BRENDAN. And you know what? – (*Rushes to the cupboard to get a baseball bat.*) I'm going to go and finish him off.

CHRISTINE. What? – No! –

BRENDAN. Might only be down the lane.

CHRISTINE. Bren –

BRENDAN (*grabbing the bat*). I'm going to batter him properly.

CHRISTINE. Think of my party.

BRENDAN. I won't have trespassing.

CHRISTINE. Alright, I've got an idea –

BRENDAN. I'll fucking kill him this time –

CHRISTINE. – how we can stop her getting to the baby.

Beat. BRENDAN *stops.* CHRISTINE *talks calmly, trying to soothe him.*

That's all you want, isn't it? Of course it is.

So –

She goes to get her toolkit from the cupboard.

So we'll just put a wee lock on the door, will we?

BRENDAN. A lock?

CHRISTINE (*looking in the toolkit*). Aye, I'm sure there's something in here we can use.

BRENDAN. And –

And only I'll have the key?

CHRISTINE. Only you'll have the key. What d'you think of that?

BRENDAN. Yeah, I like it, Mum. I like it.

CHRISTINE. But you've got to promise to keep your head down, from now on, okay?

Don't draw any more attention to us. Be calm and careful and let my party go smoothly, and we'll not hear any more about this silly / bloody –

LIV. Silly what?

LIV has come in. She is wearing her coat. Stuffed into the pocket is the rabbit toy that NAZ gave her.

Doing some DIY? Can I help?

CHRISTINE. No.

LIV. Just trying to *pull my weight.*

But if you don't need me I'm going upstairs.

BRENDAN. To the nursery?

LIV. Oh, course not.

BRENDAN. Good.

LIV. See you later –

BRENDAN. Cos we're locking it up.

Beat.

LIV (*laughs*). You're –

Why?

BRENDAN. To protect the baby.

LIV. From what?

BRENDAN. Intruders.

CHRISTINE. Aye, keeping things safe.

LIV. 'Intruders'?

BRENDAN. People like you.

Beat.

LIV. I don't know what you're talking about –

BRENDAN. Mum knows you been in there.

LIV. I haven't.

BRENDAN. Yeah? – So who left the mobile on on Wednesday?

LIV. You hearing music again, Bren?

BRENDAN. Changed his socks last night? Tidied his clothes?

LIV. Er – elves?

BRENDAN. And this morning I found this – (*The storybook.*) *open* on the floor.

Beat.

LIV. Alright.

Alright, so I went in there. Just a couple of times.

BRENDAN (*to* CHRISTINE). You see?

LIV. I've talked to him, read him a story, that's all. But – (*She goes to* CHRISTINE, *excited.*)

But you know what, Mum? – He loved it!

He smiled at me! I think he likes me!

CHRISTINE. I doubt that.

LIV. No, but he's not scared of me, you know that? – You were wrong.

CHRISTINE. Oh, *I* was wrong?

LIV. I've sat with him, and stroked him when he cried –

BRENDAN. She's fucking *touched* him?

LIV. And played with him, with this – look – (*Shows* CHRISTINE *the rabbit toy.*)

And he thinks it's hilarious – the little weirdo thinks it's really funny.

Last night I was just watching him sleep, and he didn't mind at all. Isn't it brilliant?

BRENDAN. No.

LIV. You know what it means, Mum? I could start looking after him myself.

BRENDAN. Ha! You hear that?

LIV. And if you could just show me how to pick him up, proper now, you know –

CHRISTINE. No, Liv –

LIV. How to hold him – stop him crying –

BRENDAN. That's my job.

LIV. Then I won't mess up again, I swear.

CHRISTINE. It's out of the question. You cannot handle that baby.

LIV. But I really think I / can –

CHRISTINE. And you will not go in that nursery unsupervised again.

LIV. Oh, come on – this isn't fair –

CHRISTINE. The door will be locked from now on. And only Brendan will keep the key.

LIV (*laughs*). What?

BRENDAN. Only me.

LIV. This muppet?

BRENDAN. Yeah, *this* fucking muppet.

LIV. This is a joke, right? The man who still needs you to tuck him in at night –

BRENDAN. Oi, that's not / true –

LIV. Who can't tie his shoelaces? Who can't even *think* without picking his nose?

BRENDAN. I can so.

LIV (*laughing*). Look at the state of him –

CHRISTINE. There's nothing the matter with him.

LIV. – he's been clearing up after the dogs –

BRENDAN. Er, that's not their blood –

LIV. – and he can't even change his own top.

BRENDAN. – it's a man's.

Beat. She stops laughing.

LIV. What?

What man?

CHRISTINE. Nothing. Never mind.

BRENDAN. Bloke I found in the yard.

LIV. I don't understand –

BRENDAN. Trespassing.

CHRISTINE. It was nothing.

BRENDAN. I gave him a firm warning.

LIV. What did you do?

BRENDAN. Oh, let me *think* –

With CHRISTINE*'s back turned, puts the bloody finger up his nose.*

CHRISTINE. Liv, it was nothing at all.

LIV. Oh my God –

CHRISTINE. A bit of a scuffle. He hardly touched him.

LIV. 'Scuffle'? Mum –

CHRISTINE. Now we'll put the lock on today. Only he will have the key.

LIV. No – God no –

CHRISTINE. And we'll not hear any more about this.

LIV. Mum – are you mental? You can't do that.

BRENDAN. She can.

CHRISTINE. Why ever not?

She goes to CHRISTINE, *trying to speak out of* BRENDAN*'s earshot.*

LIV. Look at him, for fuck's sake –

He's not safe to look after a child. He's lost it –

CHRISTINE. Oh, don't be melodramatic.

LIV. He's dangerous. He's just sliced up a stranger –

CHRISTINE. He was trying to defend us.

LIV. And he's only going to get worse. You know what he's like when there's a party –

CHRISTINE. I don't know what you mean.

LIV. Wound up.

CHRISTINE. You're being silly.

LIV. Aggressive.

CHRISTINE. He's a good, loyal boy. He just saw red.

LIV. That's all he ever sees these days.

CHRISTINE. Brendan's a natural with that child. You know that.

LIV. *I'm* a natural with him.

CHRISTINE. I mean, yes, he's – passionate. But sometimes that's what being a parent is all about.

He's got a gift.

BRENDAN. I've got a gift.

LIV. He's got a temper. And he's unpredictable. What if he loses it again?

CHRISTINE. He'd never hurt that baby.

LIV. He'd hurt anything that gets in his way. And you know what? – No –

I won't have him in that nursery any more.

BRENDAN. Well, it's not up to you.

LIV. You can't lock me out. You can't let him go in there.

BRENDAN. I can. And I will.

LIV (*to* CHRISTINE). Tell him –

BRENDAN (*pointing at the rabbit*). And I'll take that thing with me, if he likes it so much.

Give it me.

LIV. No.

CHRISTINE. Liv, give him the stupid toy.

LIV. No, I never will.

BRENDAN *tries to snatch the rabbit toy. It falls on the floor and they both scramble for it.* BRENDAN *gets there first.* LIV *tries to grab it back but* BRENDAN *takes out a flick knife and points it at her.*

BRENDAN. Sorry, did you want this?

LIV. Yes.

BRENDAN. Oh. Okay.

BRENDAN *puts the toy on the table and stabs it repeatedly, tearing at it. He stops, laughs at* LIV*'s horrified expression. Then throws it back to her –*

You know what, I've just decided. You been so naughty, you won't have Saturday mornings from now on. Not till next month.

No, fuck it – until Christmas.

He runs out, upstairs. CHRISTINE *goes back to her toolkit. She has prepared a drill and a padlock. Outside, it is starting to rain.*

LIV. Please, Mum, you've got to put a stop to this now.

CHRISTINE. 'Got to', is it?

LIV. He only listens to you. You need to control him –

CHRISTINE. And you need to remember your place, young lady.

You are an arrogant little child and I won't be told what to do by you.

LIV. He's violent –

CHRISTINE. 'Violent'? And was it Brendan who shook that baby like a fucking rag doll? Made it wail in pain –

LIV. I wasn't trying to hurt / him.

CHRISTINE. – or was it Brendan who walked in and / stopped you?

LIV. Oh God, won't you ever let me forget it?

CHRISTINE. No, Liv, I'm here to remind you of your biggest fucking failure – just like you remind me of mine, every single time I see you –

Beat. CHRISTINE *tries to calm herself.*

So. The Brummies –

The Brummie boys confirmed that they'll join us, did you hear?

All down to me, of course. My negotiating skills.

So we need to let the others know. I was going to send your brother to do a wee ring-around but – (*Looking out at the rain.*) Perhaps I'd like to send you out instead.

LIV. No. Don't send me out there. Don't send me out now or / I'll –

CHRISTINE (*laughs*). Or what?

LIV. You don't know what I could do.

CHRISTINE. What? – Throw a wee tantrum, like you always did? And threaten to tell on me to your daddy?

No – I think, today, you need a little reminder of who's boss.

LIV. Daddy's the boss.

CHRISTINE. But Daddy's not here right now, is he?

LIV. –

CHRISTINE (*she gives* LIV *the list*). There. Use the phone box in town and don't let anyone see your face. Destroy it when you're finished, you know the drill. Oh, and don't breathe a word about this business with Brendan. Not to anyone, understand? Or next time I'll let him slice up anything he likes.

CHRISTINE *turns to go out, upstairs, taking the tools. The rain batters the roof.*

Take your time. No one will be missing you here.

Alone, LIV *is distraught. She takes the rabbit toy out of her pocket.* BRENDAN *has torn a great hole in it, and stuffing is creeping out. She claws at it angrily, tugs out the fluff, until she finds –*

NAZ*'s number, screwed up, hidden inside. She runs out.*

CHRISTINE *returns, carrying a pretty floral dress on a hanger, and some make-up. She goes to the window to check that* LIV *is gone. She throws on the dress then quickly puts on make-up. Meanwhile, banging and drilling begin upstairs, as* BRENDAN *starts to fit the nursery lock.*

She suddenly notices the finger lying on the table. She goes and picks it up. She glances upstairs, in the direction of the drilling. A brief look of concern...

But this is interrupted by a knock on the front door. She hurriedly clears the finger away, throwing it out the back window to the dogs. Then runs to the front window and looks out.

When she realises who it is, she beams a wide, excited smile.

Scene Seven

An hour later. LIV *and* NAZ *in the park again, sheltering from the rain.* NAZ *is holding a children's rucksack with some of his daughter's toys in it.* LIV *is very agitated, angry.*

NAZ. You said it was / urgent.

LIV. Fucking – don't rush me –

NAZ. Rush what? You got something to say?

LIV. –

NAZ. You rang me.

LIV. I know, I know, I was pissed off –

NAZ. About what?

LIV. I can't –

I don't –

NAZ. Look, if you want to talk, that's great – but I'm late to pick up my daughter –

LIV. Yeah?

NAZ. It's fine, I don't mind, / but can you just –

LIV. From school, you mean? I bet she's good at school.

NAZ. What?

LIV. Bet she's a clever little girl if you want her to be a / vet.

NAZ. Liv –

LIV *(babbling)*. I want mine to be a park ranger – I think he'd like it, you know, being outside, looking after all the animals they got in here – feeding them and cleaning them out and playing with them – or maybe like a zoo- / keeper –

NAZ. Liv, please – why did you ring me?

Beat.

LIV. I don't know. I don't know. Just –

Tell me more.

NAZ. About what?

LIV. If I help you. If I tell you when it's happening and you bust into / this party –

NAZ. We talked about this –

LIV. – you'll take my mum and my brother.

NAZ. We'll take everyone who's there.

LIV. Charge them with what, though? – If they're just hanging out –

NAZ. With being present at a dog fight.

LIV. And then what? For my mum?

NAZ. You know.

LIV. Prison? Tell me.

NAZ. Possession of illegal breeds. Keeping a premises for dog-fighting –

LIV. How long for?

NAZ. – possession of dog-fighting equipment –

Good few months.

LIV. But not my dad. You wouldn't stop his parole.

NAZ. If he's not involved, he's not involved. When's it happening?

LIV. And about this refuge place. You promise we'd be safe there.

NAZ. I told you everything.

LIV. I mean, it sounds nice and that but it's not home, is it?

NAZ. Look, the offer's not going to be around for ever –

The team's getting impatient and they want to make a move.

LIV. I know but this is all –

NAZ. If you don't want to get done as an accessory you got to give me / something.

LIV. – this is all too fast.

NAZ. It's not. It can happen. You can just go home right now and pick up the kid –

LIV (*laughs*). No, I can't.

NAZ. And I'll come and collect you tonight.

LIV. I can't do that.

NAZ. Say you're going to the shops or something –

LIV. You don't understand.

NAZ. Make an excuse. Walk out of there –

LIV. No.

NAZ. Just pick him / up and –

LIV (*louder*). No, I can't do that. I can't even –

NAZ. –

LIV. I can't even pick him up.

   You see? So how could I – ?

   Beat.

NAZ. What d'you mean? Course you can pick him up.

   LIV *shakes her head.*

LIV. He wails. He hates me.

NAZ. Don't be daft, he's your kid.

LIV. But I fucked up, so bad. I had him and I – *shook* him and I –

NAZ. Right.

LIV. Oh, not much, not much, but he went pale, and *screamed*, and
   I thought he was dying, and I didn't know – I mean, I don't /
   know –

NAZ. Okay.

LIV. – what to do with him, / cos –

NAZ. Alright, alright.

   Beat.

   Well, look, it's not rocket science, is it? I'll show you –

LIV. What d'you mean?

NAZ. You can have this –

He takes the rabbit toy from LIV *and lies it down on the floor.*

And I'll borrow something of Salima's –

He pulls out a rag doll from his daughter's bag, sits on the floor near it.

Sit here.

LIV (*laughs*). I can't –

NAZ. Do you want me to help you or not?

LIV. People are looking –

NAZ. Never mind them. Watch.

She sits. He has laid the toy rabbit on the floor in front of LIV. *And the doll is in front of him.*

So imagine this is the baby, yeah? When they're little, it's just –

LIV. People are looking at me –

NAZ. – one hand, open wide, like this, underneath his neck. Support his head, that's the heaviest bit. Do it.

LIV *does it.*

Good. And the other hand under his arse. Yeah.

And then just lift him, gently. And roll him into the corner of your arm. Okay?

LIV. I'm doing it wrong.

NAZ. No, you're not – that's good, that's fine.

So, do it again. Hand under head, hand under back – and roll –

She does it.

Yeah, there you go. Piece of piss.

When he's a bit older, you know, you can pick him straight up –

Yeah, like that. But you still got to mind the head, mind the head. And if he's yelling –

LIV. Yeah, he yells like blue murder –

NAZ. Then you can, like, move him onto your shoulder or some-thing.

LIV *tries it.*

Exactly, yeah. Or you can hold them close, and sort of sway –
slow –

That's it, that's really good.

LIV (*pleased*). Is it?

NAZ. It's just about confidence, see. Don't be nervous, or he'll
sense that.

You're the one in charge. You're the grown-up here.

LIV (*swaying with the 'baby'*). I'm –

Yeah.

NAZ. Good, you got it – like you're slow-dancing with him, like –
(*He demonstrates.*)

LIV *watches him, laughs.*

What's the matter?

LIV. Long time since you've been slow-dancing, is it?

NAZ. I'm divorced, what d'you expect?

LIV. I'm sorry, I'm sorry. Joke.

(*Laughs.*) Look at the state of you –

*He is standing with the kid's rucksack on his back, cradling the
rag doll. She laughs. She stops. Beat.*

NAZ. Liv. Please. Tell me when the party is.

LIV. –

NAZ. So you made a mistake with him – so what? I've made
some –

I mean, some huge mistakes, but –

Beat. She remains silent, still. He waits as long as he can, then –

Okay. Well, I tried, didn't I?

Putting the doll back in the bag, preparing to go.

I got to go, I'm late –

LIV. Don't leave me –

NAZ. I'm sure you'll be okay. You got the rabbit to look after you.

Although looks like that's on its last legs.

LIV. Oh, no, don't say that. He loves this stupid thing.

He thinks it's hilarious, you know – the floppy ears –

NAZ. Yeah, well. Babies are weirdos.

LIV (*laughs*). They are, yeah, that's what I said.

Except I don't really mind cos when he laughs it makes me feel like – I don't know –

Like I've done something –

Good.

And I'd do anything, to hear that. You know what I mean?

NAZ. Yeah, I know.

You can try this instead then –

He gives her the doll that he was practising on.

LIV. Oh, no – you can't give me that –

NAZ. She's too old for it now.

She'd want you to have it.

LIV (*takes the toy*). Thank you.

NAZ. No worries. Good luck then.

LIV. Stay one more minute –

NAZ. Take care.

LIV. Please –

NAZ. Bye.

LIV. It's Monday.

He stops.

It's Monday night.

She takes the contact list from her pocket and holds it out. He takes it, opens it, reads.

NAZ. Pack a bag.

LIV. Don't come near the house. You've got to swear you won't /
come near –

NAZ. I won't, I promise.

I'll meet you back here in two hours. Yeah?

She nods.

Scene Eight

CHRISTINE *is in the backroom with* DANNY. *He is sitting at the
table in front of an empty plate – he's just finished a homecoming
meal. His bag is nearby.*

DANNY. So, you didn't even tell her?

CHRISTINE. I didn't want to get her hopes up, you know, in case
this didn't happen –

DANNY. You knew it was happening.

CHRISTINE. Aye, well maybe –

Maybe I just wanted you to myself for a little bit – (*She tries to
kiss him.*)

DANNY (*turning from her*). I've got some washing in here.

He opens his bag and starts sorting through.

CHRISTINE. I've got a surprise for you, actually. A homecoming
treat.

DANNY. What's that then?

CHRISTINE. Something I think you'll really like.

I organised it all / myself –

DANNY. Spit it out, Christine.

CHRISTINE. A party.

DANNY. –

A party? Or a *party* party?

CHRISTINE (*laughs*). What d'you think?

DANNY. You've organised – ? *You?*

CHRISTINE. I wanted you to have a treat. I wanted to show you –

DANNY. When is it?

CHRISTINE. Monday. All the usual lads are coming. Stevie, Gary, Paul, Keith –

DANNY. Richie?

CHRISTINE. Aye. And –

And some new boys, as well.

DANNY. What sort of new boys?

CHRISTINE. Gary put me on to these lads in Birmingham. Asians, it is. They're mad for it there.

DANNY. I don't want strangers here.

CHRISTINE. Oh, they're not – not now. I went up to watch some action with them, and they're great boys. Proper dog-men.

DANNY. They won't know our rules –

CHRISTINE. I told them everything.

DANNY. There's not room in here –

CHRISTINE. I cleared the training stuff out of the garage – we can have it there.

DANNY. I can't get the dogs fit by Monday. We've not started on the keep –

CHRISTINE. But we've been working Rex and Steel every day. Running your log book to the letter.

You should see Rex on the treadmill now – an Olympic bloody sprinter he is.

And his work on the flirt poles – God, I'm so fucking proud! – The lad's got jaws like a shark, I'm telling you.

We're going to put on a show they'll never forget. It's all ready to go.

And I've done it all myself. Aren't you –

Pleased?

Beat. He smiles.

DANNY. Aye, I've missed the party life.

CHRISTINE. And this'll be the biggest ever. More people, more money.

And you know what that means?

DANNY. Fireworks.

CHRISTINE. We can grow the business, Danny. You and me, together, can make it bigger than it's ever been.

DANNY. 'Bigger'? What d'you mean?

CHRISTINE. These Brummie boys, they're just the beginning. They got links in Manchester –

Glasgow – Liverpool –

We could hold proper conventions. Expand the yard.

DANNY. Oh, I don't know –

CHRISTINE. Start a proper kennels, with more dogs, cos –

Beat. She's excited.

Danny, there's this breeder, from Helsinki – I met him in Birmingham.

He had a prospect for sale – fucking beautiful pup – albino pit. Son of a grand champion. Already rolled, and perfect gameness, so I –

I cut a deal to buy him.

DANNY. You did what?

CHRISTINE. And a bargain price. I got him down to eighteen grand!

DANNY. Christine – it's not up to you to be cutting deals –

CHRISTINE. I said we'd go out to pick him up, next week. Have a nice long holiday while we're there.

DANNY. I've only just got home –

CHRISTINE. A second honeymoon, though – wouldn't you like that? Romantic wee log cabin in the woods. Just us / two –

Offstage, the front door opens.

LIV (*offstage*). Hello?

CHRISTINE. Liv –

LIV (*offstage*). Mum, I got to go out again. I need to take the
baby –

DANNY (*whispering, excitedly*). Get her in here.

CHRISTINE. Come in a second, please.

LIV (*entering*). – look I know you said I wasn't allowed to touch
him / but I think he needs –

LIV *comes in to the room. She is drenched from the rain, dishev-
elled, upset. She sees* DANNY, *standing with his arms open to
her. For a moment she is frozen in surprise and disbelief.*

Dad?

DANNY. How are you, puppy?

LIV. Oh my God. You're here. You're really here!

*Delighted, she runs into his arms. He gives her a massive hug,
two years in the making.*

What happened?

DANNY. Good behaviour.

CHRISTINE. But I didn't want to raise your / hopes, so –

LIV. Oh God – thank God –

Hugs him again, then:

There's someone I want you to meet. Your grandson – (*She tries
to lead him away.*)

DANNY. Aye, I heard about him.

LIV. Come on, come and / see him.

DANNY. No, I don't want to, Liv, alright?

Things to do. I hear we've got a party to get ready for.

Beat.

LIV. Oh –

DANNY. Monday night.

LIV. Yeah –

DANNY. You know about it?

CHRISTINE. Course she knows.

LIV. Yeah, I just –

CHRISTINE. Liv's just been to do a final ring-around.

LIV. – forgot, for a minute –

DANNY. Fucking great surprise, isn't it?

LIV. Yeah.

DANNY. Could be a hell of a show. As long as we can keep
security tight.

LIV (*nervous*). Why – why would security not be tight?

DANNY. Oh, you know. Cos of these new boys your mum's asked
to come.

CHRISTINE. I told you, I've vetted them all –

DANNY. And I've just got out. There'll be eyes on me.

CHRISTINE. Love, we've got to get on with our lives.

LIV. But – like you / say –

CHRISTINE. Think of the future.

LIV. If it's risky –

Maybe we should cancel.

CHRISTINE (*laughs*). You hear this? After all my work?

LIV. If you don't think it's safe –

DANNY. Don't worry, pup. I'm sure your mum's been thorough.

CHRISTINE. Low-key and last-minute. I'm a professional.

DANNY. And our contact list's as safe as ever. Christine?

CHRISTINE. All locked up in here, where you left it – (*She taps
her head.*)

Apart from – you know – Uncle Paddy Corrigan. We let him out
sometimes.

55

DANNY. Ha, I'd forgotten about him. So the peelers still swallowing that?

CHRISTINE. Never the sharpest.

LIV. Daddy –

DANNY. Liv, don't I deserve a good homecoming? And you a good birthday.

LIV. –

You remembered.

DANNY. Of course I remembered. Monday's an important day, isn't it?

The most important day of my life.

Well, the second most, after Rex's birthday.

He laughs, encouraging LIV *to smile. Beat.*

God, look at you, did you swim here? Let's dry you off. Christine, go and get her some towels.

CHRISTINE. She can go / herself –

DANNY. Now, please.

CHRISTINE *goes upstairs.* LIV *and* DANNY *face each other. There is too much to be said.*

LIV. I'm so –

I'm so sorry – Daddy –

DANNY. The baby? Aye.

You let me down there, you know.

LIV. I've been stupid –

DANNY. You have that.

Hey – but would you know what Mum said? That you'd gone and got up the shoot on purpose.

LIV. Oh God – I wish I'd never –

DANNY. Exactly, I mean, why would you do that? The fucking mouth on that woman, when it was her who let you run off on heat like that in the first place.

LIV. I'm sorry –

DANNY. Come on, though – don't be upset. What's done can't be undone, can it?

And now Daddy's here to cheer you up, amn't I?

LIV. –

DANNY. Now, did you say you were away out again tonight? When you came in –

LIV. Erm – yeah –

DANNY. Don't go, though, eh? Stay with me and we'll have a night in.

Watch an old film. Chew the fat. Just you and me.

LIV. Yeah.

DANNY. Oh aye, and there's something very important we got to get back in training for.

DANNY steps towards her and motions as if he's playing 'Paper Scissors Stone'.

One – two – three – (*Then he makes his hands into dogs' claws.*)

LIV (*smiles*). You still remember that?

DANNY. Course. Should have seen me getting the lads inside to play it – thought I was away in the head. Come on then. One – two – three –

They play together. This time LIV gestures 'dog', DANNY gestures 'money'. They freeze. She smiles.

Ha. You got me. Dog takes money. Again?

This time, DANNY makes a dog. LIV mimes baseball bat. She smiles.

LIV. I win. Baseball bat beats dog – (*She mimes this.*)

DANNY. Er, if it's Rex, no fucking chance. My boy is unbeaten.

LIV (*smiles*). You can't make up the rules, Daddy.

DANNY. It's my game, isn't it?

I can make up any rules I like.

She smiles. They play again.

Scene Nine

Two days later. Sunday evening. LIV, CHRISTINE, *and* DANNY *are in the backroom.*

CHRISTINE *is at the table. There are four chairs. Between two opposite places,* CHRISTINE *is laying a candle on the table – the places are intended for her and* DANNY.

LIV *is by the front window, looking out anxiously. She is texting on her mobile.* DANNY *has just arrived with a big paper bag of food from a McDonald's Drive-Thru.*

BRENDAN *is outside in the yard. There is a commotion out there – the dog barking over the sound of kids' party music ('The Hokey-Cokey').*

DANNY (*unpacking the food*). Christine, I hope you still like a Big Mac.

CHRISTINE. The bigger the better.

DANNY. Right, yeah. And for the kids – (*Takes two Happy Meals from the bag.*)

Liv, who you texting?

LIV. What? No one –

DANNY. Come on then, come and eat.

LIV. I'm not hungry.

DANNY. Nerves, it it? About tomorrow. All those people coming for your birthday?

LIV. –

DANNY. I hope you've something pretty to wear.

LIV *shakes her head.*

Daddy'll find you something then, don't worry.

He pulls a chair back at one of the 'grown-up' places.
CHRISTINE *assumes it's for her, until –*

Liv. Sit.

LIV *obediently goes to sits in the chair, and he tucks her in. He sits in the opposite place himself.*

Christine, go and fetch that eejit, will you?

CHRISTINE *goes out the back door.*

LIV. Daddy, listen – about tomorrow night. Don't you think we should have some kind of –

Escape plan.

DANNY. Remember when you used to save me these wee toys?

LIV. In case we need to evacuate. I mean, if – if there was a fire –

DANNY. We don't need an escape plan, puppy. Everything's under control. Trust me.

LIV. Yeah, except –

DANNY. What's the matter with you? Always used to love a party.

LIV. Did I?

DANNY. What's changed?

BRENDAN *bursts in through the back door, with* CHRISTINE *following. He is carrying the stereo, blasting out music. He is upbeat and happy. There is a key around his neck – the key to the nursery – and a baby monitor clipped to his belt.*

BRENDAN. Mental! D'you see Rex?

Spoiling for it! Music makes him flip – watch this –

CHRISTINE. Sit, Brendan, please.

BRENDAN *goes to the window so he can see the dog in the yard. He turns the music right down. Outside, the dog quietens. Then he turns the music right back up again. The dog goes mad.*

BRENDAN. Look at that – I've got him jumping like a fucking ballerina.

He'll walk it tomorrow. Make Mum her twenty grand before he's even broke a sweat. And if that tramp comes back we can just pay / him off –

DANNY. Tramp? What tramp?

CHRISTINE. It's nothing.

DANNY. Was someone / here?

CHRISTINE. No, he's just – (*Mimes 'mad'.*) you know. Brendan. Sit.

BRENDAN puts the stereo on the side, and comes to sit down. The whole family are seated now.

BRENDAN. I reckon I might become the actual best handler in the actual world.

I've realised now. That's my destiny.

Cos I know I'm not the sharpest fucking tool in the box, but I'm still – you know – a tool, aren't I?

DANNY. You said it, Bren.

BRENDAN. Tomorrow night, I want to be your right-hand man, Dad.

DANNY. Aye? Why the sudden flush of enthusiasm?

BRENDAN. I've got to think of the future now. Get myself a career. For my kid –

LIV (*quietly*). He's not your kid.

BRENDAN. He is so. Mum said I've got a gift.

That boy's got to have some proper footsteps to follow in.

One day, him and me, we're going to take over this business from you and Mum.

DANNY. This is my business, not your mother's.

BRENDAN. And my son will be the fiercest handler, everyone's scared of him.

He can punch through walls. He can vandalise ten men at once. And he can break people's arms with one fist because I've trained / him to –

DANNY. Enough about the fucking baby.

LIV (*gets up from her seat*). I feel sick.

BRENDAN. Yeah, everyone's going to feel sick when they see what he can do.

She goes back to the window and watches. DANNY *keeps his eyes on her.*

So tomorrow night, no more of that 'Wait by the door, Brendan,' 'Fetch stuff, Brendan,' 'Hand out the coke, Brendan.' I want to do bag checks when people arrive.

DANNY. Fine.

BRENDAN. Then I want to be Rex's handler for the night.

DANNY (*laughs*). You've got to be joking.

BRENDAN. Why not?

DANNY. You think I'm going to trust a kid with a forty-grand dog?

BRENDAN. I'm not a kid –

DANNY. No chance.

BRENDAN. Alright then, I want to be our watcher during his bout.

DANNY. Your mum will do that.

BRENDAN. Timekeeper.

DANNY. Richie.

BRENDAN. Or handle disposals. Let me take care of the losers.

DANNY. No, no, I'll be doing any dispatches myself.

CHRISTINE. Oh, but maybe you could help him, Bren. You know, work-shadowing.

BRENDAN. Where you going to do it?

DANNY. I'll need a mains supply –

CHRISTINE. Oh, no – Danny, please –

DANNY (*to himself*). Maybe an extension out to the yard –

BRENDAN. What for?

CHRISTINE. Stick to the Tandragee bath, for Christ's sake. No more electrical experiments –

BRENDAN. What electrical experiments?

DANNY goes to a cupboard. He takes out a sports bag, opens it. He pulls out a device made of tangled electrical wires. On one end, a three-pin plug. On the other, the wire splits and connects to two giant crocodile clips. He displays it, proudly, looking to see if LIV *is watching.*

DANNY. You've seen this around, eh? Liv?

BRENDAN. Yeah, but I don't get it.

DANNY. One clip on an ear. One on the tail – (*He demonstrates using the Happy Meal box.*)

Twenty fucking amps and a bucket of water on their heads –

BRENDAN. And it works? You've tried it?

CHRISTINE. What d'you think blew the wiring in this place?

BRENDAN. Oh, please let me do it. Dad –

DANNY. No, no.

BRENDAN. Please, I want to learn.

DANNY. Maybe Liv can do it.

BRENDAN. Her?

DANNY. Seems a bit shy at the moment, but she always used to help out.

LIV. Oh, no, I –

BRENDAN. See, she doesn't want to. I do.

DANNY (*to* LIV). Why not?

BRENDAN. I'll do it. Daddy, give me a chance –

DANNY. Bren, it takes guts to finish off a dog.

BRENDAN. I got guts. I got loads of them.

DANNY. Liv?

BRENDAN. Come on, I've got more bloody guts than that little slag.

CHRISTINE. Brendan –

BRENDAN. You think it was that thing that blew the electrics? It wasn't, it was her – fucking that lad from school in the fuse cupboard on the last day of term – wasn't it, Liv? – (*A snort of laughter.*)

CHRISTINE. Brendan, stop.

BRENDAN. – trying to get up the duff so she can get a council flat. I heard her tell him.

Yeah – hey, Mum – reckon that's when the sparks really flew?

BRENDAN *laughs, then realises too late that he's said the wrong thing.* DANNY *puts down the device.*

DANNY. How dare you talk about your sister like that?

BRENDAN. Come on, it's just a joke, isn't / it –

DANNY. We don't do jokes in this house. Go out to the garage and we'll have a talk.

BRENDAN. What?

DANNY. I'll come to you there. Go on.

CHRISTINE. There's no need for / that, Danny.

DANNY. Now, Brendan, please.

BRENDAN. I'm sorry, I didn't / mean it.

DANNY. Go.

Upstairs, the baby starts crying. Beat, as they all hear it. Then BRENDAN *stands up from the table, taking the key from around his neck.*

BRENDAN. No – see, I've got to go and check on him.

DANNY. Go outside, now.

LIV. I'll see to him then.

DANNY. No you will not.

LIV. Give me the nursery / key.

BRENDAN. He's calling to / me.

LIV. He is / not.

BRENDAN. I love him / more.

LIV. No, you don't and you never / will –

DANNY (*louder*). Shut up! Shut up. No one is going up to the little shit.

You will both go out to the garage and wait for me there, and there'll be no more talk about the wretched baby.

And I will have the nursery key from now on.

I will have all the fucking keys in this place. Give it, Brendan.

BRENDAN *hands over the key.* DANNY *takes a bigger bunch of keys from his pocket and attaches it.*

Now off you go outside, both of you.

LIV. Daddy –

Why me? What have I done?

DANNY. Oh, nothing, puppy, nothing.

But I want you to learn. (*To* BRENDAN.) Because if anyone's going to run this business when I'm gone, it's her – not you and that little intruder.

You understand that, you fucking retard? Go.

They both go out. The baby's crying continues. DANNY *starts to search around for something – in the cupboards, under the stairs offstage…*

That wee shit can fuck off if it thinks she'll come running.

CHRISTINE. Danny –

DANNY. She didn't even want him, and now he's making demands.

CHRISTINE. Danny, don't let them wind you up. They're disobedient brats, all three of them.

DANNY. Where's my fucking – ?

CHRISTINE. Did you think about Finland? We could get away from them there.

Maybe stay for a / while –

DANNY. Christine, where's my knuckleduster?

CHRISTINE. I chucked it.

DANNY. You what? So what am I meant to use now?

CHRISTINE. I don't know – I'm sorry –

Look, this new prospect we're buying –

DANNY. Jesus, Christine, we're not getting a new dog. It's a ridiculous idea.

CHRISTINE. What?

DANNY. You can tell whoever it is that the deal's off.

CHRISTINE. But – why?

DANNY. Because you shouldn't have made it in the first place. You don't know anything about buying a dog.

CHRISTINE. I do, I've learned, and –

If you don't want to train him, I'll do it.

DANNY. Ha. You?

CHRISTINE. I'll be his handler.

DANNY. You're not a handler, Christine, you're a housewife.

CHRISTINE. No, come on, I can be.

I can train dogs. I can hold fights –

DANNY. You can cook, you can clean, and you can whelp.

CHRISTINE. Danny, please, let's work together. Buy me that dog –

DANNY. I don't need a business partner –

CHRISTINE. – and I'll show you what I can do.

DANNY. – I've got Liv. She's all I need. That's it.

CHRISTINE. That's not it. It can't be it. Tomorrow night, when the money's in your hand, you'll think again. You're forgetting, I know how to persuade you –

She goes to him and kisses him. He is fired up, turned on, and he lets her. As she kisses him more passionately, she leans in and undoes the buckle on his belt. He helps her. Then, he slides the belt out of his trousers, and pulls away from her.

DANNY (*pulling the belt tight across his fists*). Aye, that'll do. I won't be long.

He goes out to the garage. She stands, alone.

Scene Ten

The next night. The night of the party.

In the Party House, the garage at the bottom of the driveway, things are in full swing. Inside, in the back room, there are balloons hanging up, streamers, and a banner saying 'Happy 18th Birthday ~~Brendan~~ Liv'. There's an entryphone system newly installed beside the back door, to allow communication between the house and garage.

LIV is sitting at the front window, staring out nervously. She is wearing the floral dress that CHRISTINE wore earlier. She fiddles with it uncomfortably.

CHRISTINE and BRENDAN enter through the back door. BRENDAN now has a bruised face. He is carrying a crate of empty beer bottles. CHRISTINE is carrying something heavy, in a black bin bag – the bleeding body of a dead puppy. She takes it through, out to the kitchen offstage, then returns.

BRENDAN. I thought these sort weren't meant to drink.

LIV. Shouldn't you be refereeing?

BRENDAN. Dad put me on 'fetching stuff' instead.

He dumps the crate, finds a big stash of cocaine, which he stuffs into his pockets. Meanwhile, CHRISTINE goes to the cupboard and takes out the waterproofs that we saw her put on in Scene Two. They are clean. She puts them on.

Started with the juniors. Richie's new thing fought one the Brummies brought.

Fanged itself three times but it got torn to bits in the end.

Steel's up now. Dad's got seven grand on him.

Everything okay out the front?

LIV. Fine.

BRENDAN. Daddy said you should come in and watch Rex's bout, next.

Give you some hokey-cokey if you want, as it's your birthday. Coming?

LIV *shakes her head.*

Please yourself.

He goes. CHRISTINE *and* LIV, *alone. She looks at* LIV *in the dress.*

CHRISTINE. It doesn't suit you. Not one bit.

LIV. I didn't choose it.

Mum, you know that, don't you – ?

The buzzer on the wall rings suddenly. CHRISTINE *picks up the receiver.*

CHRISTINE (*into the phone*). Aye, Danny, I'm coming, I'm coming.

Glances at LIV.

No. She doesn't want to.

She hangs up. She goes.

A long pause. LIV *paces, anxious. The sound of a car passing, outside. She rushes to the window, expectantly. But moments pass, and nothing, no one, materialises.*

A shout goes up from the Party House, another contest has been won. It distresses LIV *and she looks for something to distract herself. She goes to the cupboard and finds a bag, hidden secretively. From it, she takes the battered rabbit toy. It has a needle and thread in it, half mended. She picks it up and, with shaking hands, tries to sew.*

Then. A tap on the front window. LIV *instinctively ducks. Then looks out, realises it's* NAZ. *She throws down the sewing and shouts to him, gestures.*

LIV. Go away! Fuck off!

She pulls the blind, but he taps on the window again. He won't go. LIV *checks the back window to make sure there's no one watching from the yard. Then runs to answer the front door. She returns with* NAZ. *She locks the back door and pulls down the back-window blind.*

NAZ (*seeing the decorations*). It's your birthday?

LIV. Why have you come? I texted you –

NAZ. You didn't turn up to meet me. Have they started?

LIV. Yeah.

NAZ. Get the baby then. Quick.

LIV. So where's the rest of them?

NAZ. They're following.

LIV. You're not with the 'team'?

NAZ. I came to get you. They don't know I'm doing this.

LIV. Oh yeah?

NAZ. They'll be ten minutes. Let's go.

LIV. No.

NAZ. We need to get the baby / out –

LIV. You're not listening –

NAZ. Have you packed?

LIV. No. Leave me.

NAZ. What?

LIV. I can't come with you.

NAZ. Stop pissing around –

LIV. I'm not. I don't want to. I'll stay here and it'll be fine.

NAZ. You don't mean that –

LIV. Go now, alright? Or I'll warn them that you're here.

NAZ. Come on, you won't.

LIV (*rushing to the entryphone*). I will. I'm telling / them –

NAZ. No, don't. Don't. Please.

What's the matter with you?

LIV. I know you won't help me. I know you're a liar.

NAZ. I don't understand –

LIV. I rang the police station yesterday.

I wanted to tell you things had changed.

NAZ. So?

LIV. I told them at the front desk who I was. I thought they'd know me.

NAZ. Liv –

LIV. The big investigation.

NAZ. We haven't really got time for / this –

LIV. But they'd never heard of me.

And they said you weren't even there any more. You were suspended.

Not leading a case at all.

Beat.

NAZ. Okay, okay –

LIV. So this is just a hobby then, is it?

NAZ. No –

LIV. You lied to me.

NAZ. Can we talk about this later?

LIV. Or never. Go on, fuck off.

NAZ. Look, I had to do this.

LIV. You made me think –

NAZ. And I didn't lie to you – I am a police officer – I'm just –

I fucked up –

LIV. 'Fucked up' what?

NAZ. I made a stupid mistake. I didn't help someone who I should have.

I go to a misconduct board in two weeks, and I don't –

I don't want my daughter growing up knowing I chucked my whole career away. I thought if I could bring them a rock-solid case they might wipe the slate clean –

LIV. So you haven't got a team?

NAZ. I have. Once you told me the plans I went to them –

LIV. They're not 'right behind you'.

NAZ. We got a warrant. They're on their way.

LIV. But –

But you can't take me to that place, can you?

NAZ. I can. I will.

Look, I've come for you, haven't I?

They told me to leave you. They said you'd had your chance. But I've come for you.

LIV. –

NAZ. I know you want to do this.

LIV. I'm scared.

NAZ. I know. But what you could have –

It's worth being scared for.

A tap on the back window.

DANNY (*outside*). Liv? Liv!

LIV. My dad!

NAZ. I thought he was inside.

LIV. You've got to go now.

NAZ. No.

DANNY (*outside*). Liv? What's going on?

NAZ. Just tell him the truth. Tell him you want to leave.

LIV. I can't.

DANNY (*outside*). Liv!

LIV. He'll kill me.

NAZ. He'll kill me first, I'm sure.

LIV. If I don't let him in he'll batter the fucking door down.

NAZ. Let him in then, go on. I'll fill time till they get here.

LIV. You can't –

NAZ. I know what to say, don't worry.

DANNY (*outside*). Liv!

NAZ. Be brave, go on.

She lets DANNY in. He is excited, keyed up. He is leading Rex, a pit bull. As he talks he ties him up in the corner. NAZ hangs back, and DANNY is so breathlessly excited that he doesn't notice him at first.

LIV. Sorry, Daddy.

DANNY. Steel fucking wrecked the other thing!

LIV. That's great.

DANNY. Twenty-four fucking minutes, it's a record.

Takes a wad of cash from his pockets and counts the money, delighted.

Look at this – look at all this! Fourteen from Steel, five from the pups, and a bit from Brendan's wee sideline. How long since you held twenty grand, puppy?

Rexy here's up next and I got seven on him. But I want you to have the rest – (*He divides up the money and thrusts a load of it into LIV's hands.*) take it.

LIV. What? No –

DANNY. Aye, it's yours. We can do that extension we used to talk about. A flat on the side of the house so you can –

He notices NAZ. Beat.

LIV. This is –

This is –

NAZ. I'm Liv's friend.

DANNY. 'Liv's *friend*'?

NAZ. Hello.

DANNY. I didn't think Liv had any friends.

NAZ. Well. Yes, actually. She has me.

Don't you, Liv?

Beat.

LIV (*smiles*). Yes.

NAZ. And I just came to say happy birthday.

DANNY. Well, it's not the best time, I'm afraid. So if you wouldn't mind going.

NAZ. No, you don't understand, I'm –

DANNY. Liv'll show you out.

NAZ. I'm here for the party.

Beat. LIV *looks increasingly scared. She goes to the front window to look out for the team.*

You know what I mean.

DANNY. Her party?

NAZ. Yeah. Actually.

DANNY. You've been invited, have you?

NAZ. I've come a long way for this.

DANNY. You're one of the Brummie boys?

NAZ. Right.

DANNY. I thought they were all here already.

NAZ. I got lost.

DANNY (*to* LIV). Is this right?

NAZ. Course it's / right –

DANNY. Liv, is this right?

LIV. Erm. Yeah.

DANNY. You're sure? He's one of us –

LIV. Of course I'm sure, Daddy.

DANNY. Of course. Okay. (*Relaxes.*) Well, I'm – Danny. I'm in charge here.

NAZ. I've heard a lot about you.

DANNY. And you can drop that 'friend of Liv's' act now. We're safe.

NAZ. Oh – right –

DANNY. No worries on that front, tonight.

I'm sorry, didn't mean to be unfriendly just there.

I should have known that you were one of them. I mean you're –

Aren't you? – (*Doing a little bow.*) Inshallah.

NAZ. Right.

DANNY. I'm afraid we've started already.

NAZ. No problem.

CHRISTINE (*in the yard, approaching*). Danny?

DANNY. You're in time for the third round though. Hope you've got your pocket money.

NAZ (*showing him his wallet*). Plenty of it.

DANNY (*pleased to see the money*). Aye, good man.

CHRISTINE *and* BRENDAN *come in. The waterproofs*
CHRISTINE *put on are now splashed with blood.* BRENDAN
is carrying a baseball bat.

CHRISTINE (*coming in*). Danny – we're waiting for you –

DANNY. Hmm?

BRENDAN. Who's that?

DANNY. One of the Brummies. Got lost.

CHRISTINE. I thought they were all here.

DANNY. It's fine, Liv vouched for him.

BRENDAN (*suspicious*). Where's his dog then?

NAZ. Oh –

I didn't bring him. Injury.

BRENDAN. Yeah? So what's his name?

DANNY. He's fine, Brendan, he's fine. Relax.

Take some more beers in and I'll be there in a minute.

Christine, wipe them down, will you, you look a state.

(*To* NAZ.) I'm sorry about this. I don't want you to think we're a bunch of yobs –

NAZ. Fine. Take your time – (*Looking at* LIV, *at the window*.) Take your time.

DANNY. If you're going to come in to the party I need to check – you know –

NAZ. –

DANNY. Your pockets.

NAZ. Oh – yeah, sure.

BRENDAN *puts the baseball bat on the table and starts filling up a crate with more beers*. CHRISTINE *finds a cloth and tries to clean down her overalls*. LIV *is at the window, anxiously watching the road. Meanwhile* NAZ *turns out his pockets for* DANNY *to check. As they do this they continue talking.*

DANNY. I'm sorry to hear about your dog.

NAZ. Yeah, it's fine, I'll patch him up. He's a winner.

DANNY. Sorry we didn't get to meet him then. What's his weight?

NAZ. Thirty-seven pounds.

DANNY. Good size. Date of birth?

NAZ. 7th January, 2007.

DANNY. Where d'you get him?

NAZ. Erm –

Finland.

DANNY. Thought your lot would get them shipped from Pakistan.

NAZ. Oh. Well, yeah. But I prefer the Finnish stock.

DANNY. Aye? My wife too.

NAZ. Yeah? (*Pleased he's saying the right thing, he relaxes a little.*) I mean, there's some top-class breeders out there.

DANNY. Apparently. So you must have met some of these Helsinki lads.

LIV. Dad, stop asking questions.

DANNY. What's the matter?

LIV. You're bombarding him.

DANNY. Ach, you know the way it is. It's just nice to find someone with like-minded interests.

NAZ. Absolutely. We're being hunted all the time, aren't we?

DANNY. By people who don't understand the sport.

NAZ. Exactly.

DANNY. So who else d'you know in the circuit? Over here?

NAZ. Oh – not many –

DANNY. But you've been to parties before? You do go to parties – conventions –

NAZ. Yeah, yeah, of course.

DANNY. So. Who've you partied with?

LIV. You don't have to answer that.

NAZ. No, it's fine.

DANNY. I'm sorry, I don't mean to quiz you, / it's just –

NAZ. Like I said, it's fine. Course I been to parties. You know, with –

Paddy Corrigan.

Beat. The family stop what they're doing. BRENDAN *slowly reaches for the baseball bat.*

DANNY. Paddy – ?

NAZ. Sorry, 'Uncle' Paddy Corrigan, isn't it?

BRENDAN. I thought that / was the –

CHRISTINE. Shut up, Brendan.

NAZ. You – know him?

DANNY. Oh aye, we know him. How d'you get to meet Paddy then?

NAZ. I – I can't –

DANNY. Liv probably introduced you, did she? If you're a friend of Liv's –

LIV. Naz –

NAZ. Oh, yeah, that's right. Yeah, I remember now –

DANNY. And you get on with Paddy?

NAZ. House on fire, yeah. He likes me.

DANNY. Nice guy, isn't he?

NAZ. Top guy.

DANNY. Very trusting.

LIV. Daddy – listen –

DANNY. Shush, Liv, please. Shush now.

NAZ. Lot of – tattoos. I think –

DANNY. Tattoos? Oh aye. If I remember rightly, there's one across his chest, saying:

'My heart belongs to Daddy.'

NAZ. I wouldn't know.

DANNY. You remember that one, puppy?

LIV. –

Beat.

DANNY. Well. All this fucking chatter. We're not getting on with the business in hand.

You can go in to the party now.

NAZ. Oh – right, yeah.

DANNY. If you're sure that's what you're here for.

NAZ. Course I'm sure. Can't fucking wait.

DANNY. Good. Brendan and Christine here will show you where to go.

BRENDAN. But, Dad, he's –

DANNY. He's our guest. And you know where to take him.

He hands BRENDAN *the sports bag containing the electrical leads.* BRENDAN *puts down the bat and takes the bag instead, realising what* DANNY *means. He is excited.*

BRENDAN. Course I do. Fucking – fireworks!

LIV. Naz, don't / go –

NAZ. No, no. It's fine. That's what I'm here for, isn't it?

See you later.

BRENDAN *leads* NAZ *out.* CHRISTINE *follows.* LIV *goes to the window to watch.* DANNY *stands with her.*

DANNY. So what is he, pup? A reporter? A cop?

LIV. Daddy –

DANNY. Can't be a cop, they don't come in that colour. Did he pay you?

LIV. No.

DANNY. Blackmailed then, was it?

So what d'you want me to do to the little cunt?

LIV. Nothing. Don't hurt him.

DANNY *(laughs)*. Oh, come on –

LIV. Let him go.

DANNY. Puppy, maybe you don't understand. I'd do anything –

CHRISTINE *comes back in, carrying a bucket. She goes through the room, offstage to the kitchen, to fill it with water.*

– anything you asked me to, to keep you safe and happy – d'you know that?

From the night you were born, pups, I knew.

I'd protect you from anyone who intruded, and I'd rage –

I'd fucking *rage* against anything that tried to hurt you.

I'd burn down the world for you and make it again, just how you wanted it, if only you asked me to. I'd rip the heart out of life, and put it in your hands.

Because I love you so much, Liv, it's –

Fierce inside me. It howls when you're not there.

CHRISTINE *creeps back in with the full bucket of water, and hears him –*

See your mum, she clings to me like a fucking dying leech. Sucking up all the time.

Brendan, he clings to anything that'll give him some love. But you –

You're all backbone. And sometimes I see that I made something so strong, and bright, and brave, and that almost makes me feel –

Good.

I'd fight to the death for you, puppy, you know that? I'd do anything.

(*He points out of the window.*) So look at him, there, and tell me what you want me to do for you now.

LIV. Daddy –

DANNY. I know it's not pretty – but you're a brave girl, come on. You can say it.

LIV. I want to leave.

I want to leave home.

Beat. CHRISTINE*'s ears prick up.*

DANNY. You – ?

I don't understand –

LIV. Cos – all those things, Daddy. I don't want them.

You can't hurt people cos of me. You can't tear the heart out of anything, or anyone.

And I don't want –

I don't want you to fight for me, any more. Cos I can fight for myself.

And I got a reason to do that, now. You understand?

Beat.

DANNY. Aye.

Of course. *The baby.*

LIV. He needs me.

DANNY. He's your priority.

LIV. I think so, yeah. And I got to go.

DANNY. –

Your timing's not great, you know that? The middle of a fucking party.

CHRISTINE. The middle of my party.

DANNY. But then I suppose that was the idea, was it? While we were distracted.

LIV. I'm sorry.

DANNY. Without saying goodbye. Get your friend out there to come for you, is it?

LIV. Daddy, you asked what I wanted –

DANNY. Aye, and you want me to let him go. And you.

Cos you'll be wanting to get on the move – I should help.

LIV. You don't have to –

DANNY. I'll go and pack a bag for you.

LIV. It's fine –

DANNY. No, let me do this one thing, puppy, before you go.

Christine, can you stay here with her, please?

CHRISTINE. Brendan needs this water –

DANNY. Leave it. I suppose we'll have to free him, anyway, if he's Liv's friend.

LIV. Thank you, Daddy.

CHRISTINE. But he's seen too much –

DANNY. Then I'll ask him, nicely, not to say anything.

CHRISTINE. We should break up the party –

DANNY. No, no, don't cause panic. It's under control now, isn't it?

Just leave him out there, wait here, and I'll be down in a minute.

Come on, Rexy.

He goes out, taking Rex with him. LIV *and* CHRISTINE *alone.*

LIV. I'll –

I'll still come and visit you, Mum. If you want.

CHRISTINE. Thank you, Liv, but I don't need you to pity me.

Your daddy and me are off on holiday, actually, next week.

LIV. He didn't tell me that.

CHRISTINE. A romantic break. And he's going to buy me my own dog.

LIV (*laughs*). You? A dog?

CHRISTINE. Champion in the making. And a bargain price.

LIV. I thought we were broke –

CHRISTINE. Not after tonight. We've made twenty grand already.

LIV. Yeah, I know / but –

CHRISTINE. And he'll put that on Rex of course, and win again, and then we're laughing.

We'll go out there together and we'll spend some time alone. Pick up the dog.

And then we'll come home and build this business together –

LIV. He's not going to do all that.

CHRISTINE. Equal partners.

LIV. He's not going to buy you a dog.

CHRISTINE. He will. Now we've got the / capital –

LIV. He gave the winnings to me.

CHRISTINE. –

LIV. He gave it to me.

CHRISTINE. I don't believe you.

LIV. You're an idiot, Mum –

She produces the money from her pocket. She puts it on the table. CHRISTINE *looks at it, sadly. Then* DANNY *returns. He is carrying a suitcase. He dumps it at* LIV*'s feet.*

DANNY. Well then. There we go. That what you wanted?

LIV. Daddy, thank you for being so understanding.

DANNY. Of course, Liv. You're my baby girl. I understand everything about you.

He takes out his bunch of house keys and locks the door that leads to the stairs.

LIV. I was just telling Mum, I'll come and visit whenever you –

(*As he locks it.*) What are you doing?

DANNY (*as he hands the key to* CHRISTINE). Christine, I need you to stay here with her.

LIV. Sorry, can you open that?

DANNY. I think I'm wanted out there with Brendan, aren't I?

LIV. I need to go upstairs to the baby.

DANNY. No, puppy, you don't.

LIV. Of course I do. I've got to get him ready to go.

DANNY. You're not leaving.

LIV. What? But you just said you / understood –

DANNY. I understand what you *think* you want.

But I'd like you to think again in a couple of minutes.

LIV. A couple of minutes? What d'you mean?

DANNY. You're my child, not his mother.

LIV. Where's –

DANNY. You need to stay here with me.

LIV. Daddy, where's the dog?

DANNY. I think you'll be able to see everything more clearly, without the brat.

LIV (*starting to panic now*). He was in here with us –

DANNY. You'll be able to see where your priorities really lie.

LIV. Dad, where's – ? Dad – ?

DANNY. I shut him in the baby's room.

Beat.

LIV. What?

CHRISTINE. Danny – no –

DANNY. Don't worry, Liv, Rex is my dog –

LIV. Oh my God –

DANNY. He'll take care of him. You know what I mean.

LIV. No – God no –

DANNY. It'll be like an accident, okay? Then we can all go back to / normal.

LIV. Let me out – let me up / there –

DANNY. It's all for you. You said you wished you'd never had him.

LIV. Please – Daddy –

DANNY. And now you don't.

Keep her in here for a bit, Christine. Five minutes should do it.

CHRISTINE. Danny, I don't think this is a good idea.

LIV. Daddy – please – / please –

CHRISTINE. He's a little shit but he doesn't / deserve this –

LIV. I don't want you to do this / for me –

DANNY. You'll obey me, Christine. You hear?

Now sit.

CHRISTINE *sitting, in shock*.

(*To* CHRISTINE.) Good. And keep her in here.

LIV. No, you've got to let me out – oh God –

DANNY *picks up the bucket of water and goes out to the yard.*

LIV *tries desperately to force the door.*

CHRISTINE. Maybe you should sit down too.

LIV. Sit down?! Are you mad? Let me go –

CHRISTINE. I can't. Daddy said –

   LIV *gives up trying to force the door and rushes to*
   CHRISTINE.

LIV. Mum, please – don't listen to him.

CHRISTINE. I have to.

LIV. You don't. Give me the keys, come on.

CHRISTINE. You don't understand. He's all I've ever had –

LIV. So?

CHRISTINE. I think I'd fight to the death for him, Liv.

LIV. Yeah, and he'd let you. And be happy that you did it.

   And chuck your body on the heap with all the other mutts.

   Mum, you know you're worth more than that. Please.

   Upstairs, the baby starts crying.

   Oh God – Mum –

   Just do something good – for once –

   Beat. CHRISTINE *puts the key in the lock and opens the door.*
   LIV *is about to dash out –*

CHRISTINE. Liv –

   She hands LIV *the baseball bat.* LIV *takes it and runs upstairs.*

   *There is a commotion in the yard, offstage, and suddenly the
   lights fizz out. The fuses have blown again with a surge of elec-
   tricity outside. At the same time, from upstairs, the baby crying,
   and the dog barking.* CHRISTINE *is about to run to the fuse
   box when she hears –*

   *The sounds of the raid. Police storm the Party House, running,
   shouting. Breaking up the show.*

   CHRISTINE *runs to the window and looks out, then ducks
   down. The buzzer on the wall rings repeatedly, violently.*

CHRISTINE *runs to it and is about to pick it up, then –*

Sees the money on the table. She stops. Considers.

Then quickly she pulls her waterproofs off and dumps them on the floor. She takes the money. She leaves by the front door, quickly.

Suddenly, the cacophony is over. There's an eerie silence in the house. And the lights come back on. After a moment, NAZ *rushes in. He is wet. He searches desperately for* LIV. *He can't see her.*

Then he hears her coming down the stairs. He freezes and waits.

She emerges. She is carrying a silent baby, and the baseball bat. She is covered in blood. Some of it's hers – from bites on her arms and legs and face – some of it's the dog's. Her clothing is torn.

She and NAZ *stand facing each other, both breathless, as at the beginning.*

NAZ *looks at her, expectantly.*

The baby starts crying, and she rocks it. She kisses it.

Black.

The End.

A Nick Hern Book

Breed first published in Great Britain as a paperback original in 2010 by
Nick Hern Books, 14 Larden Road, London W3 7ST, in association with
Theatre503

Breed copyright © 2010 Lou Ramsden

Lou Ramsden has asserted her right to be identified as the author of this work

Cover image: iStockphoto.com
Cover designed by Ned Hoste, 2H

Typeset by Nick Hern Books, London
Printed in the UK by CLE Print Ltd, St Ives, Cambs, PE27 3LE

A CIP catalogue record for this book is available from the British Library

ISBN 978 1 84842 145 5

FSC
The mark of responsible forestry
TT-COC-003115
FSC Trademark © 1996 Forest Stewardship Council A.C